At Issue

Marijuana

Other Books in the At Issue Series:

At Issue

Marijuana

Arthur Gillard, Book Editor

GREENHAVEN PRESS
A part of Gale, Cengage Learning

GALE
CENGAGE Learning

Detroit • New York • San Francisco • New Haven, Conn • Waterville, Maine • London

GALE
CENGAGE Learning™

Christine Nasso, *Publisher*
Elizabeth Des Chenes, *Managing Editor*

© 2009 Greenhaven Press, a part of Gale, Cengage Learning.

Gale and Greenhaven Press are registered trademarks used herein under license.

For more information, contact:
Greenhaven Press
27500 Drake Rd.
Farmington Hills, MI 48331-3535
Or you can visit our Internet site at gale.cengage.com

Articles in Greenhaven Press anthologies are often edited for length to meet page requirements. In addition, original titles of these works are changed to clearly present the main thesis and to explicitly indicate the author's opinion. Every effort is made to ensure that Greenhaven Press accurately reflects the original intent of the authors. Every effort has been made to trace the owners of copyrighted material.

Cover image © Images.com/Corbis.

LIBRARY OF CONGRESS CATALOGING-IN-PUBLICATION DATA

Marijuana / Arthur Gillard, book editor.
   p. cm. -- (At issue)
  Includes bibliographical references and index.
  ISBN 978-0-7377-4432-3 (hbk.)
  ISBN 978-0-7377-4433-0 (pbk.)
  1. Marijuana--United States--Juvenile literature. 2. Marijuana--Therapeutic use--Juvenile literature. 3. Marijuana--Law and legislation--United States--Juvenile literature. I. Gillard, Arthur.
  HV5822.M3M2675 2009
  362.29'5--dc22
                               2009010710

Printed in the United States of An
1 2 3 4 5 6 7 13 12 11 10 09

362.29
MAR
2009

Gillard, Arthur.
Marijuana

Contents

Introduction

Marijuana has been in use for at least five thousand years, and perhaps much longer, first in Asia and gradually spreading throughout the world. For much of that time it has been used primarily to produce rope and clothing, but has been employed for a variety of other uses as well: as medicine, religious sacrament, food, as a treatment for addiction to other drugs, and even as a punishment for criminal wrongdoing. Jack Herer explains, "The most serious punishment/ rehabilitation meted out in many African tribes for capital crimes was forcing the transgressor to smoke or consume massive amounts of cannabis non-stop for hours on end in a small, enclosed hut until he passes out—literally unconscious from inhaling the fumes. The equivalent of a year or two's supply for a heavy American smoker is consumed in just an hour or so. Does it work? African users say the rate of repeat criminal offenses after dagga [marijuana] treatment is virtually non-existent."

In addition to these uses, marijuana often had unsavory connotations as well. Nearly a thousand years ago hashish (a concentrated form of marijuana) was reputedly used as an enticement to recruit assassins. According to Ted Gottfried in his book *The Facts About Marijuana*, "Legend has it that hashish was named after Hasan-ibn-Sabah, the head of a murderous sect. . . Hasan's stronghold was a training camp for assassins who were promised entry to paradise in exchange for serving him. Recruits were escorted to a garden where they were given hashish and entertained by sensual and obliging dancing girls. Afterward they were brought to Hasan, who promised them more visits to the garden if they carried out his orders." The Christian Inquisition banned use of marijuana in Spain in the twelfth century and France in the thirteenth, and in the fourteenth century the Emir (Islamic ruler) Soudon Sheikhouni similarly prohibited the substance in India.

In the twentieth century the use of marijuana as a recreational, mind-altering substance became much more widespread than had previously been the case. In the 1920s, when alcohol was prohibited in the United States, use of the drug spread through the subculture associated with jazz music. E.J. Sana informs us that during this period, "unlike the speakeasies (clubs that featured alcohol), police left marijuana clubs alone, because the people who visited did not become rowdy (like drunks did), and the drug was not illegal."

By the time alcohol prohibition ended in 1933, however, marijuana was increasingly seen as a dangerous threat to a well-ordered society, fueled by sensational media reports associating it with madness, criminality, and sexual immorality— and soon marijuana was itself prohibited in America. Despite ever more vigorous attempts to control it, use of the drug continued to increase throughout the 1950s and became strongly associated with the countercultural revolution of the 1960s. While more progressive elements of society advocated marijuana legalization, more traditional elements saw it as a threat to social stability and were concerned about negative health consequences, addiction, and its possible role as a "gateway drug" leading to use of harder drugs.

At the same time interest in other uses of marijuana—as food, fuel, fabric, and especially medicine—expanded dramatically, and in the 1980s individual states began to legalize medical marijuana in the face of entrenched opposition by the federal government. As a result of the ongoing struggle over the fate of marijuana in modern American society, much research has been conducted into possible harmful effects of its use, and while the results of such research remain controversial and contested, research into beneficial uses of marijuana—as well as its psychoactive constituents (known as "cannabinoids") or similar chemicals (referred to as "analogs")—is showing some promising results. For example, in a report given to the U.S. Drug Enforcement Administration in 2005, Lester Grinspoon testified, "The new [cannabinoid] analog Dexanabinol (HU-211) has been shown to protect brain cells (in animals) from damage when given immediately after a stroke."

In twenty-first-century America, the marijuana debate continues to become more complex and nuanced. Some people would like to see marijuana available as a medicine but not as a recreational substance. Others, including an increasing number of conservatives, consider the drug war to be too ineffective, costly, and antithetical to personal liberty to be worth continuing—however they may feel *personally* about marijuana use. Still others consider it important for society to oppose marijuana use on general moral principles, even if the drug war is ultimately unwinnable.

The issue continues to be of paramount concern to the American people. Reporting on the Obama administration's Web-based poll asking citizens to vote on what issues are of most pressing concern, National Organization for the Reform of Marijuana Laws (NORML) deputy director Paul Armentano noted on January 13, 2009, "Of the more than 76,000 questions posed to Obama by the public, the fourth most popular question overall called on the administration to cease arresting and prosecuting adults who use cannabis. And in the subcategory 'National Security,' the most popular question posed by the public pertained to amending U.S. drug policies as a way to try and halt the ongoing violence surrounding illicit drug trafficking in Mexico and other nations."

The authors of *At Issue: Marijuana* present diverse views on the many facets of this complex and ongoing debate. Whether marijuana's harms outweigh it's benefits, and what place, if any, it may legitimately occupy in modern American society, is an issue that has yet to be decided.

1

Marijuana Is Dangerous

U.S. Drug Enforcement Administration

The U.S. Drug Enforcement Administration (DEA) is the federal agency responsible for enforcing America's drug laws.

If marijuana is legalized, great harm to children and society will result—especially considering the greatly increased potency of the drug today. Adolescents are particularly vulnerable to marijuana addiction, and marijuana use often leading to the use of more dangerous drugs. Depression, suicidal thoughts, and schizophrenia have been linked to marijuana, and many physical health problems also may result from its use, including damage to the brain and lungs. In addition, many behavioral problems and risky behaviors result from use of marijuana, ranging from serious fights in school to fatal car accidents.

Legalization of marijuana, no matter how it begins, will come at the expense of our children and public safety. It will create dependency and treatment issues, and open the door to use of other drugs, impaired health, delinquent behavior, and drugged drivers.

This is not the marijuana of the 1970's; today's marijuana is far more powerful. Average THC [tetrahydrocannabinol, the main psychoactive substance found in the cannabis plant] levels of seized marijuana rose from less than one per cent in the mid-1970's to a national average of over eight per cent in 2004. And the potency of "B.C. Bud" [cannabis grown in British Columbia, Canada] is roughly twice the national average—ranging from 15 per cent to as high as 25 per cent THC content.

U.S. Drug Enforcement Administration, "The DEA Position on Marijuana," November 20, 2008.

Marijuana Dependency and Treatment

- Adolescents are at highest risk for marijuana addiction, as [according to a 2004 article in the *Seattle Post-Intelligencer*] they are "three times more likely than adults to develop dependency." This is borne out by the fact that treatment admission rates for adolescents reporting marijuana as the primary substance of abuse increased from 32 to 65 per cent between 1993 and 2003. More young people ages 12–17 entered treatment in 2003 for marijuana dependency than for alcohol and all other illegal drugs combined.

Marijuana is a frequent precursor to the use of more dangerous drugs, and signals a significantly enhanced likelihood of drug problems in adult life.

- [According to the Office of National Drug Control Policy:] "[R]esearch shows that use of [marijuana] can lead to dependence. Some heavy users of marijuana develop withdrawal symptoms when they have not used the drug for a period of time. Marijuana use, in fact, is often associated with behavior that meets the criteria for substance dependence established by the American Psychiatric Association."

- Of the 19.1 million Americans aged 12 or older who used illicit drugs in the past 30 days in 2004, 14.6 million used marijuana, making it the most commonly used illicit drug in 2004.

- Among all ages, marijuana was the most common illicit drug responsible for treatment admissions in 2003, accounting for 15 per cent of all admissions—outdistancing heroin, the next most prevalent cause.

- In 2003, 20 per cent (185,239) of the 919,833 adults admitted to treatment for illegal drug abuse cited marijuana as their primary drug of abuse.

Marijuana as a Precursor to Abuse of Other Drugs

- Marijuana is a frequent precursor to the use of more dangerous drugs, and signals a significantly enhanced likelihood of drug problems in adult life. The *Journal of the American Medical Association* reported, based on a study of 300 sets of twins, "that marijuana-using twins were four times more likely than their siblings to use cocaine and crack cocaine, and five times more likely to use hallucinogens such as LSD."

- Long-term studies on patterns of drug usage among young people show that very few of them use other drugs without first starting with marijuana. For example, one study found that among adults (age 26 and older) who had used cocaine, 62 per cent had initiated marijuana use before age 15. By contrast, less than one per cent of adults who never tried marijuana went on to use cocaine.

- Columbia University's National Center on Addiction and Substance Abuse reports that teens who used marijuana at least once in the last month are 13 times likelier than other teens to use another drug like cocaine, heroin, or methamphetamine, and almost 26 times likelier than those teens who have never used marijuana to use another drug.

- Marijuana use in early adolescence is particularly ominous. Adults who were early marijuana users were found to be five times more likely to become dependent on any drug, eight times more likely to use cocaine in the future, and fifteen times more likely to use heroin later in life.

- In 2003, [as cited by the Department of Health and Human Services] 3.1 million Americans aged 12 or older used marijuana daily or almost daily in the past year. Of those daily marijuana users, nearly two-thirds "used at least one other illicit drug in the past 12 months." More than half (53.3 per cent) of daily marijuana users were also dependent on or abused alcohol or another illicit drug compared to those who were nonusers or used marijuana less than daily.

- Healthcare workers, legal counsel, police and judges indicate that marijuana is a typical precursor to methamphetamine. For instance, Nancy Kneeland, a substance abuse counselor in Idaho, pointed out that "in almost all cases meth users began with alcohol and pot."

Marijuana use has been linked with depression and suicidal thoughts, in addition to schizophrenia.

Mental and Physical Health Issues

- John Walters, Director of the Office of National Drug Control Policy, Charles G. Curie, Administrator of the Substance Abuse and Mental Health Services Administration, and experts and scientists from leading mental health organizations joined together in May 2005 to warn parents about the mental health dangers marijuana poses to teens. According to several recent studies, marijuana use has been linked with depression and suicidal thoughts, in addition to schizophrenia. These studies report that weekly marijuana use among teens doubles the risk of developing depression and triples the incidence of suicidal thoughts.

- Dr. Andrew Campbell, a member of the New South Wales (Australia) Mental Health Review Tribunal, published a study in 2005 which revealed that four out of five individuals with schizophrenia were regular cannabis users when they were teenagers. Between 75–80 per cent of the patients involved in the study used cannabis habitually between the ages of 12 and 21. In addition, a laboratory-controlled study by Yale scientists, published in 2004, found that THC "transiently induced a range of schizophrenia-like effects in healthy people."

- Smoked marijuana has also been associated with an increased risk of the same respiratory symptoms as tobacco, including coughing, phlegm production, chronic bronchitis, shortness of breath and wheezing. Because cannabis plants are contaminated with a range of fungal spores, smoking marijuana may also increase the risk of respiratory exposure by infectious organisms (i.e., molds and fungi).

- Marijuana takes the risks of tobacco and raises them: marijuana smoke contains more than 400 chemicals and increases the risk of serious health consequences, including lung damage.

- According to two studies, marijuana use narrows arteries in the brain, "similar to patients with high blood pressure and dementia," and may explain why memory tests are difficult for marijuana users. In addition, "chronic consumers of cannabis lose molecules called CB1 receptors in the brain's arteries," leading to blood flow problems in the brain which can cause memory loss, attention deficits, and impaired learning ability.

- Carleton University researchers published a study in 2005 showing that current marijuana users who smoke at least five "joints" per week did significantly worse than non-users when tested on neurocognition tests such as processing speed, memory, and overall IQ.

A large shock trauma unit conducting an ongoing study found that 17 per cent of crash victims tested positive for marijuana.

Delinquent Behaviors and Drugged Driving

- In 2002, [the Department of Health and Human Services reported that] the percentage of young people engaging in delinquent behaviors "rose with [the] increasing frequency of marijuana use." For example, according to a National Survey on Drug Use and Health (NSDUH) report, 42.2 per cent of youths who smoked marijuana 300 or more days per year and 37.1 per cent of those who did so 50–99 days took part in serious fighting at school or work. Only 18.2 per cent of those who did not use marijuana in the past year engaged in serious fighting.

- A large shock trauma unit conducting an ongoing study found that 17 per cent (one in six) of crash victims tested positive for marijuana. The rates were slightly higher for crash victims under the age of eighteen, 19 per cent of whom tested positive for marijuana.

- In a study of high school classes in 2000 and 2001, about 28,000 seniors each year admitted that they were in at least one accident after using marijuana.

- Approximately 15 per cent of teens reported driving under the influence of marijuana. This is almost equal to the percentage of teens who reported driving under the influence of alcohol (16 per cent).

- A study of motorists pulled over for reckless driving showed that, among those who were not impaired by alcohol, 45 per cent tested positive for marijuana.

- The National Highway Traffic Safety Administration (NHTSA) has found that marijuana significantly impairs one's ability to safely operate a motor vehicle. According to its report, "[e]pidemiology data from road traffic arrests and fatalities indicate that after alcohol, marijuana is the most frequently detected psychoactive substance among driving populations." Problems reported include: decreased car handling performance, inability to maintain headway, impaired time and distance estimation, increased reaction times, sleepiness, lack of motor coordination, and impaired sustained vigilance.

Some of the consequences of marijuana-impaired driving are startling:

- The driver of a charter bus, whose 1999 accident resulted in the death of 22 people, had been fired from bus companies in 1989 and 1996 because he tested positive for marijuana four times. A federal investigator confirmed a report that the driver "tested positive for marijuana when he was hospitalized Sunday after the bus veered off a highway and plunged into an embankment."

- In April 2002, four children and the driver of a van died when the van hit a concrete bridge abutment after veering off the freeway. Investigators reported that the children nicknamed the driver "Smokey" because he regularly smoked marijuana. The driver was found at the crash scene with marijuana in his pocket.

- A former nurse's aide was convicted in 2003 of murder and sentenced to 50 years in prison for hitting a home-less man with her car and driving home with his mangled body "lodged in the windshield." The incident happened after a night of drinking and taking drugs, including marijuana. After arriving home, the woman parked her car, with the man still lodged in the wind-shield, and left him there until he died.

- In April 2005, an eight year-old boy was killed when he was run over by an unlicensed 16 year-old driver who police believed had been smoking marijuana just before the accident.

- In 2001, George Lynard was convicted of driving with marijuana in his bloodstream, causing a head-on colli-sion that killed a 73 year-old man and a 69 year-old woman. Lynard appealed this conviction because he allegedly had a "valid prescription" for marijuana. A Nevada judge agreed with Lynard and granted him a new trial. The case has been appealed to the Nevada Supreme Court.

- Duane Baehler, 47, of Tulsa, Okalahoma was "involved in a fiery crash that killed his teenage son" in 2003. Police reported that Baehler had methamphetamine, cocaine and marijuana in his system at the time of the accident.

Marijuana also creates hazards that are not always predict-able. In August 2004, two Philadelphia firefighters died bat-tling a fire that started because of tangled wires and lamps used to grow marijuana in a basement closet.

2

Marijuana Is Beneficial

Lester Grinspoon

Lester Grinspoon is associate professor emeritus of psychiatry at Harvard Medical School.

In addition to recreational and medical uses, marijuana is helpful in making decisions, solving problems, and generating new ideas. Unfortunately, the vast majority of research, writing, and political and legislative activity has focused on the question of its harmfulness rather than its many beneficial properties. Due to the stigmatization of users, the large marijuana subculture maintains a low profile, and influential, well-known members of society who use the drug are understandably reluctant to be open about it. However, if more such people "come out of the closet" about their use, fear and misunderstanding of the drug will be reduced. Understanding the ways in which marijuana can enhance human experience will probably always be based on anecdotal evidence, rather than more rigorous scientific methods, but its many beneficial effects still can be convincingly demonstrated.

I was 44 years old in 1972 when I experienced [my] first marijuana high. Because I have found it both so useful and benign I have used it ever since. I have used it as a recreational drug, as a medicine, and as an enhancer of some capacities. Almost everyone knows something of its usefulness as a recreational substance, growing numbers of people are becoming familiar with its medical utility, but only practiced cannabis users appreciate some of the other ways in which it

Lester Grinspoon, "To Smoke or Not to Smoke: A Cannabis Odyssey," Dr. Lester Grinspoon's Marijuana Uses, November 20, 2008. Reproduced by permission.

can be useful. It has been so useful to me that I cannot help but wonder how much difference it would have made had I begun to use it at a younger age. Because it has been so helpful in arriving at some important decisions and understandings, it is tempting to think that it might have helped me to avoid some "before cannabis era" bad decisions. In fact, now, when I have an important problem to solve or decision to make, I invariably avail myself of the opportunity to think about it both stoned and straight.

Marijuana and Critical Self-Reflection

I cannot possibly convey the breadth of things it helps me to appreciate, to think about, to gain new insights into. But I would like to share several not too personal instances. For example, let me tell you about the worst career choice I have ever made; it was my decision to apply to the Boston Psychoanalytic Institute as a candidate for training in psychoanalysis. I began this training, which was enormously costly in both time and money, in 1960 and graduated seven years later. Although I developed some skepticism about certain facets of psychoanalytic theory during training, it was not sufficient to dull the enthusiasm with which I began treating patients psychoanalytically in 1967 (coincidentally, the same year I began to study cannabis). It was not until about the mid '70s that my emerging skepticism about the therapeutic effectiveness of psychoanalysis began to get uncomfortable. This discomfort was catalyzed by cannabis. On those evenings when I smoke marijuana it provides, among other things, an invitation to review significant ideas, events and interactions of the day; my work with patients is invariably on that agenda. This cannabis review-of-the-day is almost always self-critical, often harshly so, and the parameters within which the critique occurs are inexplicably enlarged. My psychotherapy patients, patients who sat opposite me and who could share eye contact and free verbal exchange, always appeared to be making better progress than my psychoanalytic patients. I was generally satisfied with my work with the former, and invariably at first impatient and later unhappy with the lack of progress made by patients on the couch. There is little doubt that it was the cumulative effect of these stoned self-critiques that finally, in 1980, compelled me to make the decision not to accept any new psychoanalytic patients. The subsequent decision to resign from the Boston Psychoanalytic Institute was very difficult, a little like deciding to get a divorce after more than a decade of marriage. But I have no doubt that it was the only way I could deal with this growing discomfort and rectify what was now clearly seen as a mistake. . . I am indebted to cannabis for the help it provided me in achieving the clarity necessary to arrive at this most difficult decision.

There are millions of citizens who have discovered through their own experience that [marijuana] has a large variety of uses they consider valuable.

Marijuana Enhances Creativity

Cannabis can also be used as a catalyst to the generation of new ideas. Experienced cannabis users know that under its influence new ideas flow more readily than they do in the straight state. They also understand that some are good and others are bad ideas; sorting them out is best done while straight. In the absence of an agenda, the ideas are generated randomly or as close or distant associations to conversation, reading, or some perceptual experience. It is sometimes worthwhile to have a stoned go at trying to solve a particular problem. An illustration comes to mind. In 1980, during my tenure as Chairperson of the Scientific Program Committee of the American Psychiatric Association (APA) I "invented" and then edited the first three volumes of the *Annual Review of Psychiatry,* a large book which is still published yearly by the

APA. Mindful of how much money this annual publication was earning for the APA, the chief of our sub-department of psychiatry asked me to put my "thinking-cap" on and come up with a way for the Harvard Department of Psychiatry to supplement its shrinking budget. Taking his request seriously, I smoked that night for the express purpose of trying to generate relevant ideas. Within days, at a meeting in the Dean's office, it was agreed that the idea I arrived at that evening would be pursued—the publication of a monthly mental health letter. The first edition of The Harvard Mental Health Letter appeared in July 1984 and it soon achieved considerable success as an esteemed mental health publication and a steady source of income to the Harvard Medical School Department of Psychiatry. Would the idea have come or come as easily in a straight state? Maybe.

Marijuana Users Are Stigmatized and Persecuted

All through the seemingly endless heated discourse on cannabis in this country over the last three decades, little has been said or written about its many uses. The overwhelming preponderance of funding, research, writing, political activity, and legislation have been centered on the question of its harmfulness. The 65 year old debate, which has relatively recently included discussion of its usefulness and safety as a medicine, has never been concerned with its non-medicinal uses; it is always limited to the question of how harmful it is and how a society should deal with the harm it is alleged to cause. It is estimated that 76 million Americans have used cannabis and more than 10 million use it regularly. They use it in the face of risks that range from opprobrium to imprisonment. From the time I began my studies of marijuana, 12 million citizens of this country have been arrested for marijuana offenses. The number of annual marijuana arrests is increasing, and in 2000 over 734,000 people were arrested on marijuana charges, 88 percent of them for possession. Because the government allows confiscation of property in drug cases, many have lost valued possessions ranging from automobiles to homes. Most have to undertake expensive legal defenses and some have served or will serve time in prison. Unless we are prepared to believe that all these people are driven by uncontrollable "Reefer Madness" craving, we must conclude that they find something in the experience attractive and useful. And yet there is very little open exploration of these uses with the growing exception of its value as a medicine. Even here, government officials want to mute the discussion out of a fear expressed by the chief of the Public Health Service when in 1992 he discontinued the only legal avenue to medicinal marijuana: "If it is perceived that the Public Health Service is going around giving marijuana to folks, there would be a perception that this stuff can't be so bad. . . it gives a bad signal." The government has, until very recently, refused to acknowledge that cannabis has any value, even medicinal, but there are millions of citizens who have discovered through their own experience that it has a large variety of uses they consider valuable and that the health costs are minimal.

When the many people of substance and accomplishment who use cannabis "come out," it will contribute much to the diminution of cannabinophobia.

This large population of marijuana users is a subculture, one that has been present in this country since the 1960s. Three decades ago it was an open, vocal, active, and articulate culture on and off the campus. Today it is silent and largely hidden because most users, understandably, do not want to stand up and be counted. They have more than the law to fear. Urine testing is now a fact of life in corporate America; a positive test result can lead, at the very least, to a stint in a "drug treatment" program, and at most, to the loss of a job, career destruction, even imprisonment. Users are very mindful of this minefield, and most find ways around it. Even more pervasive and in some ways more pernicious is the stigmatization attached to cannabis use. Young people often experience little of this, at least among their friends. But as they grow older and move into increasingly responsible and visible positions they become much more guarded. Many believe, correctly, that colleagues would regard them as deviant if they knew. This stigmatization is abetted by the media, which have created and perpetrated a stereotyped image of "potheads" as young, hirsute, slovenly dressed ne'er-do-wells or disreputable, irresponsible, and socially marginal hedonists who use marijuana only to hang out and party. One reason for the fierce resistance to marijuana is the fear that it will somehow taint middle-class society with the "pothead" culture.

Coming Out as Marijuana Users

There is no denying that many, especially young people, use marijuana primarily for "partying and hanging out" in the same way that many more use beer. And most non-users, until they become aware of its medical value, believe that smoking to party and hang out pretty much defines the limits of its usefulness. This stereotype is powerful, and reactions ranging from puzzlement to outrage greet claims that this party drug could be useful as medicine or for any other purposes. People who make claims about its usefulness run the risk of being derided as vestigial hippies. Under these circumstances it is not surprising that most people who use cannabis do so behind drawn curtains, alone or with others who share some appreciation of its value.

It is unfortunate that those who, from personal experience, are aware of its usefulness are so reluctant to be public about it. I believe it would be good for the country if more people in business, academic and professional worlds were known to be marijuana users. The government has been able to pursue its policies of persecution and prosecution largely because of the widespread false belief that cannabis smokers are either irresponsible and socially marginal people or adolescents who "experiment," learn their lesson, and abandon all use of the drug. That lie is unfortunately perpetuated when those who know better remain silent. It's time to let the truth come out. Just as the gay and lesbian out-of-the-closet movement has done so much to decrease the level of homophobia in this country, when the many people of substance and accomplishment who use cannabis "come out," it will contribute much to the diminution of cannabinophobia [fear of cannabis].

Not many well-known people are identified as users of cannabis. A few politicians have been outed by their enemies (one went so far as to claim that he did not inhale), and some would-be political appointments have failed because of a history of marijuana use. Occasionally a screen star, musician or professional athlete is arrested for possession. Aside from Allen Ginsberg, some popular musicians, and a few notables from the Beat and hippie movements, few people in the public eye have voluntarily acknowledged cannabis use. Except for one well-known scientist, the physicist Richard Feynman, academics have been most cautious. Feynman, by courageously acknowledging his ongoing use of marijuana, won the respect and appreciation of many and the enmity of others. Fear of "coming out" is, of course, not without foundation. As long as the present stereotyped understanding of marijuana use and its effects continues to prevail, anyone who acknowledges using it will risk being taken less seriously from then on. It is thought that potheads could not possibly be considered mature, serious, responsible, and credible. Yet only those who actually use cannabis can teach us how useful it is.

There was a time not so long ago when it was generally assumed that any use of marijuana was "merely recreational." This was certainly true at the time I wrote *Marihuana Recon-*

sidered. The chapter on marijuana as medicine (The Place of Cannabis and Medicine) was concerned with past (19th and early 20th century) and potential uses; there was no overt and little covert use of cannabis as a medicine at that time. Now, there are many thousands of patients who use cannabis medicinally. And as the ranks of these patients grow, so does the number of people who observe for themselves how relatively benign this substance is. Seventy-four percent of Americans presently believe that cannabis should be made available as a medicine; very few people would have held this belief in 1971. Currently it is generally thought that there are two generic categories of marijuana use: recreational and medical. But in fact many uses do not fit into these categories without stretching their boundaries to the point of distortion; they fall into a third category, one that is more diverse and for that reason difficult to label. It includes such disparate uses as the magnification of pleasure in a host of activities ranging from dining to sex, the increased ability to hear music and see works of art, and the ways in which it appears to catalyze new ideas, insights and creativity, to name a few. Furthermore, at its edges, which are fuzzy, there is some conflation with both medicine and recreation. Yet, the preponderance of these uses falls into this broad and distinctive third category that I call enhancement. This is the class of uses which is generally the least appreciated or understood by non-cannabis users. It is also the case that some people who use or who have used marijuana may not be aware of some if not most of the enhancement possibilities.

One category of cannabis utility that we have studied is its usefulness as a medicine. Because there is not at this time a systematic clinical literature on the medicinal uses of cannabis, James B. Bakalar and I asked patients to share their experiences with cannabis as a medicine for our book, *Marihuana, the Forbidden Medicine.* . . . We supplemented these anecdotal patient accounts with our own clinical experience and what we could glean from the medical literature. Anecdotal evidence is not as persuasive as that from double-blind placebo controlled studies, the more scientifically sound modern medical approach to the safety and efficacy of new therapeutics. As the results of such studies become available we may be compelled to modify our estimate of the clinical usefulness of cannabis. At this time, however, it is difficult to imagine that future studies will subtract much from the clinical experience-driven perception that cannabis is a remarkably versatile medicine with relatively little toxicity.

It is my intention to roughly follow the same format in the Uses of Marijuana Project. While I will attempt to illuminate the various uses of cannabis through literary accounts and by sharing some of my own experiences, the prime source of what I hope will be a fairly comprehensive understanding of the uses of this versatile drug will come from contemporary users. . . Unlike medicinal use, which will eventually be fitted with scientific costume, an understanding of those uses which fall into the category of enhancement will probably always be based on anecdotal accounts; it is unlikely that marijuana's capacity for the enhancement of sexual pleasure, for example, will ever be the subject of a modern scientific (double-blind placebo-controlled) study. However, if this ethnographic method is successful we should be able to provide a reasonably proximate picture of the varieties and value of cannabis use in contemporary society. And in so doing, we cannabis users can make a significant contribution to the demise of cannabinophobia, one of our age's most damaging popular delusions.

In the meantime, Betsy [the author's wife] and I are gradually being given the opportunity to explore another dimension of the ways in which cannabis can be valuable; we are discovering its usefulness in the task of achieving reconciliation with the aging process, including coming to terms with the inevitable physical and emotional aches, deficits and losses. Cannabis also enhances our appreciation of the time we have, now that we are both emeritus, to enjoy our children, grandchildren and friends, literature, music and travel, and our daily walks in the New England woods. Of still more importance, it helps us to realize the wisdom of Robert Browning's words, "Grow old along with me! The best is yet to be. . ."

3

Marijuana Is Addictive

Joseph A. Califano Jr.

Joseph A. Califano Jr. is chairman and president of the National Center on Addiction and Substance Abuse at Columbia University.

Marijuana is the most widely used, controversial, and misunderstood drug in America. Because today it is much more potent and addictive than in the past, it is comparable in harmfulness to other plant-based drugs such as cocaine and heroin. The number of teens in treatment programs for marijuana addiction and emergency room admissions associated with its use have increased dramatically. Research shows that marijuana withdrawal resembles withdrawal from cocaine, alcohol, and opiates. Teens who use marijuana are also much more likely to use other drugs. The harmful and addictive nature of marijuana justifies the amount of attention law enforcement gives to possession, but much more needs to be done. Teens arrested for smoking pot should be educated as to its dangers and given psychological help if needed. Parents need to appreciate the increased danger and potency of pot, and communicate clearly to their children that they strongly disapprove of its use.

One substance merits individual attention because it is the illegal drug most widely used by children and teens. And because there is so much controversy among adults about the danger of using it. That substance is nonmedical marijuana. It

Joseph A. Califano Jr., *High Society: How Substance Abuse Ravages America and What to Do About It*, Cambridge, MA: Public Affairs, 2007, pp. 119–126. Copyright © 2007 by Joseph A. Califano, Jr. Reprinted by permission of Public Affairs, a member of Perseus Books, L.L.C.

is the nation's most widely used illicit drug: More than 95 million Americans have tried it, 25 million in the past year.

The efficacy and safety, benefits and risks, of medical marijuana are matters for doctors, scientists, pharmaceutical manufacturers, the National Institutes of Health and the Food and Drug Administration (FDA), and scientists like those at the Scripps Research Institute who are examining the potential of the drug's active ingredient to stave off Alzheimer's disease. But the potential of nonmedical marijuana as a dangerous, addictive, and gateway drug is a matter of concern for children, parents, physicians, and policymakers.

Today's Marijuana Is Different

No drug is more misunderstood. For a variety or reasons, millions of today's adults and teens do not appreciate the sharp edges of smoking marijuana that belie its popular posture as a "soft" drug. Parents who used the drug in the late 1960s and the 1970s often see smoking pot as a benign rite of passage, a phase they passed through on their way to becoming business executives, lawyers, doctors, and teachers. . . .

Today's teens' pot is not their parents' pot. It is far more potent. As with most other crops, farmers have learned how to grow these plants to produce a far more powerful drug. The average levels of THC [tetrahydrocannabinol, the main psychoactive substance] jumped from less than 1 percent in the mid-1970s to more than 7 percent in 2005. The potency of sinsemilla (the highly powerful version of marijuana obtained from unpollinated female plants) over the past couple of decades doubled from 6 percent to 13 percent, with some samples hitting THC levels of 33 percent. Antonio Maria Costa, the director of the United Nations Office of Drugs and Crime, in expressing concern about the worldwide rise in marijuana use and the drug's increased potency, said, "Today, the harmful characteristics of cannabis are no longer that different from those of other plant-based drugs such as cocaine and heroin."

Today's marijuana is addictive. Nora Volkow, the director of the National Institute on Drug Abuse (NIDA) puts it bluntly: "There is no question that marijuana can be addictive; that argument is over. The most important thing right now is to understand the vulnerability of young developing brains to these increased concentrations of cannabis."

Today, the harmful characteristics of cannabis are no longer that different from those of other plant-based drugs such as cocaine and heroin.

Scientific Studies of Marijuana Addiction

Even though since 2002 overall marijuana use has been level and teen use has slightly decreased, overall use has doubled to 15 million people from its 1993 low of 7.4 million people, and at 2.6 million, teen use is more than double its 1992 low of 1.1 million. Especially troubling, the number of admissions for treatment for marijuana dependence, largely of teens, hit 300,000 in 2004, more than double the number from a decade earlier, and the number of teen emergency-room admissions in which marijuana is implicated went up almost 50 percent in just five years, from 1999 to 2004. Though alcohol (notably beer) remains far and away their drug of choice, teens are three times likelier to be in treatment for marijuana (partly as a result of drug courts) than for alcohol and five times likelier to be in treatment for marijuana than for all other illegal drugs combined.

The Collection of Scientific Studies in the 2006 Book *Cannabis Dependence* makes the case for addiction beyond any reasonable doubt. Of marijuana users, 2 to 3 percent get hooked within two years of inhaling their first joint; 10 percent of those who try it will get hooked at some point in their lives. In the decade ending in 2003, the proportion of admissions with marijuana as the primary drug of abuse more than doubled, jumping from 7 percent to 16 percent. Over this same period, the proportion of admissions citing alcohol or cocaine as the primary drug of abuse fell. In 2003, among illicit drug users, marijuana topped all others (except prescription and nonprescription opiates) as the primary drug of abuse.

The rate of addiction among daily marijuana users, as diagnosed from the fourth edition of the American Psychiatric Association's *Diagnostic and Statistical Manual* (DSM-IV), is higher than among daily drinkers. The diagnosis from the DSM-IV, the scientifically defined clinical standard for addiction, occurs when a user experiences at least three of these seven conditions: increased tolerance and diminished impact of same usage, withdrawal syndrome, greater consumption over longer periods, inability to control use, preoccupation with obtaining the drug, important work or recreational activities abandoned, continued use despite the harm it causes.

Rats subjected to immediate cannabis withdrawal exhibited changes in behavior similar to those seen after the withdrawal of cocaine, alcohol, and opiates.

The addictive nature of marijuana is also revealed by the experience of the university researchers across the country who worked on the *Cannabis Dependence* book. As part of their study, they placed advertisements in papers offering treatment to individuals unable to stop using marijuana. Hundreds responded. (The typical volunteer was a white-collar man in his thirties who smoked pot every day).

A team at the Scripps Research Institute in California and one at Complutense University in Madrid found that rats subjected to immediate cannabis withdrawal exhibited changes in behavior similar to those seen after the withdrawal of cocaine, alcohol, and opiates. *Science* magazine called this "the first neurological basis for marijuana withdrawal syndrome, and one with a strong emotional component that is shared by other drugs." At the 2006 meeting of the American Psychiatric Association (APA), Deborah Hasin, a researcher at the Columbia University School of Public Health, urged that the APA's diagnostic manual and the World Health Organization's disease classifications be updated to include "cannabis withdrawal syndrome." Research shows, she said, that heavy marijuana users who try to stop experience lethargy, insomnia, psychomotor retardation, and clinical anxiety and depression. Staying clean is just as hard for marijuana addicts as it is for heroin addicts, says Robert Stephens, chair of psychology at Virginia Tech University and one of the editors of the *Cannabis Dependence* book.

Marijuana Is a Gateway Drug

From the standpoint of protecting children, teens, and the public health, reducing marijuana use merits front-burner attention. As has been true of tobacco since the 1960s, we've learned a lot about the dangers of marijuana since the 1970s. The drug adversely affects short-term memory, the ability to concentrate, emotional development, and motor skills. These consequences are particularly damaging to teens when they are in school learning and their brains and bodies are rapidly developing. Recent studies indicate that marijuana use increases the likelihood of depression, schizophrenia, and other serious mental health problems. . . .

The White House Office of National Drug Control Policy has found that adults who were teen marijuana users are eight times likelier than those who were not to use cocaine and fifteen times likelier to use heroin. A study published in the *Journal of the American Medical Association*, which examined 300 sets of fraternal and identical same-sex twins, found that those who smoked pot were four times more likely to use cocaine or crack and five times more likely to use hallucinogens than their twins who did not smoke pot.

The Institute of Medicine report *Marijuana and Medicine: Assessing the Science Base* noted, "In the sense that marijuana use typically precedes rather than follows initiation of other illicit drug use, it is indeed a gateway drug." The report went on to say that "people who enjoy the effects of marijuana are, logically, more likely to be willing to try other mood-altering drugs than are people who are not willing to try marijuana or who dislike its effects. In other words, many of the factors associated with a willingness to use marijuana are, presumably, the same as those associated with a willingness to use other illicit drugs."

Adults who were teen marijuana users are eight times likelier . . . to use cocaine and fifteen times likelier to use heroin.

Discouraging Marijuana Use

The increased potency of today's marijuana, its addictive and gateway potential, and the greater knowledge we have of its dangers justify the attention that law enforcement is giving to illegal possession of the drug. [Mayor] Rudolph Giuliani's success in slashing New York City's crime rate by, among other things, going after low-level street crime such as smoking marijuana and selling small amounts of it inspired many other mayors to follow suit.

But the disappointing reality is that from 1993 to 2005, a 107 percent increase in marijuana arrests was accompanied by a 100 percent increase in marijuana users. Among teens, the number of users over that period more than doubled to 2.6 million. The failure of such a sharp increase in arrests to translate into even a remotely comparable reduction in use of the drug signals that something more is needed.

Like the entire substance abuse problem, the matter of preventing marijuana use is all about kids. Discouraging children and teens from getting involved with the drug begins with understanding the importance of preventing kids from becoming cigarette smokers. Most kids who smoke nicotine cigarettes do not smoke marijuana, but a 2003 survey of twelve- to seventeen-year-olds reveals that teens who smoke cigarettes are much likelier than nonsmokers to try marijuana. They are also likelier to become regular marijuana users.

Parents must understand that the drug available today is far more potent and dangerous than what they might have smoked thirty years ago.

We should seek to make public policies, including law enforcement approaches, more effective in discouraging teen marijuana use. When five million twelve- to seventeen-year-olds can obtain marijuana in an hour or less and ten million can get it within a day, reducing availability is high on the list. Beyond that—and recognizing that reducing demand is key to that goal—we should use the increased arrest rate as an opportunity to discourage use.

In the mid-1990s, while I was visiting Los Angeles, then Mayor Dick Riordan told me that in his city kids were arrested an average of nine times for possession of marijuana before anything happened to them. I have since discovered that this situation is common in many American communities. Most kids do not even get a slap on the wrist the first few times they're caught smoking a joint. As a result, we let them sink deeper and deeper into drug use, with its dangers to their physical, mental, and emotional development and its risk of addiction and harder drug use.

I am not suggesting that we put kids in jail the first time they get caught smoking pot. But why not treat a teen arrested for marijuana use much the same way we treat someone arrested for drunk driving when no injury occurs? Why not use the arrest as an opportunity and require kids cited for marijuana possession to be screened psychologically and referred for help if appropriate, and to attend sessions to learn about the danger of marijuana use and how to decline the next time they are offered a joint? The incentive to be screened and attend such classes would be the threat of the alternative: for the first couple of arrests, loss of a driver's license or a fine stiff enough to sting that has to be paid by the teen or worked off; for continued use, intensive treatment, including random testing and staying clean to avoid jail time. Getting kids to attend sessions designed to discourage their marijuana use would give some practical meaning to increased law enforcement and would bring reductions in drug use more in line with increased arrest rates. The certainty of swift punishment can not only discourage use but can also be a powerful incentive for these kids to attend classes or get needed treatment.

These steps will help, but we will never be able to arrest our way out of the teen marijuana problem. Parents are the first line of defense. Parents must understand that the drug available today is far more potent and dangerous than what they might have smoked thirty years ago. For their children, smoking marijuana is not a harmless lark but a dangerous experiment that can bring serious harm and may end up destroying their lives. When parents understand that and make it clear to their children that they strongly disapprove of any marijuana use, that will discourage their kids from using the drug.

4

Marijuana Is Not Addictive

Paul Armentano

Paul Armentano is the senior policy analyst for the National Organization for the Reform of Marijuana Laws, which aims to legalize marijuana and supports the development of a regulated market for the drug.

A great deal of federal money is available to researchers studying marijuana addiction. Much media attention is devoted to the topic, and large pharmaceutical companies hope to make a lot of money treating it. However, it is doubtful that marijuana is addictive in any meaningful sense. Most people in treatment programs for marijuana addiction are there because they've been ordered to attend following arrest for possession. Unbiased research casts serious doubt on the idea as well, showing that marijuana dependence is less likely and less severe than that associated with other drugs such as alcohol and nicotine. Withdrawal symptoms, when they occur, are mild and subtle compared to the severe effects of withdrawal from alcohol or tobacco. Although a small percentage of marijuana users may find quitting difficult, this does not justify putting it in the same legal category as heroin, nor arresting 800,000 Americans annually for pot violations.

The U.S. government believes that America is going to pot—literally.

Earlier this month, the U.S. National Institute on Drug Abuse [NIDA] announced plans to spend $4 million to estab-

Paul Armentano, "Setting the Record Straight on Marijuana and Addiction," LewRock well.com, November 20, 2008. Reproduced by permission of the publisher and author.

lish the nation's first-ever "Center on Cannabis Addiction," which will be based in La Jolla, Calif. The goal of the center, according to NIDA's press release, is to "develop novel approaches to the prevention, diagnosis and treatment of marijuana addiction."

"Marijuana Addiction" Is Big Business

Not familiar with the notion of "marijuana addiction"? You're not alone. In fact, aside from the handful of researchers who have discovered that there are gobs of federal grant money to be had hunting for the government's latest pot boogeyman, there's little consensus that such a syndrome is clinically relevant—if it even exists at all.

But don't try telling that to the mainstream press—which recently published headlines worldwide alleging, "Marijuana withdrawal rivals that of nicotine." The alleged "study" behind the headlines involved all of 12 participants, each of whom were longtime users of pot and tobacco, and assessed the self-reported moods of folks after they were randomly chosen to abstain from both substances. Big surprise: they *weren't* happy.

According to state and national statistics, up to 70 percent of all individuals in drug treatment for marijuana are placed there by the criminal justice system.

And don't try telling Big Pharma—which hopes to cash in on the much-hyped "pot and addiction" craze by touting psychoactive prescription drugs like Lithium to help hardcore smokers kick the marijuana habit.

And certainly don't try telling the drug "treatment" industry, whose spokespeople are quick to warn that marijuana "treatment" admissions have risen dramatically in recent years, but neglect to explain that this increase is due entirely to the advent of drug courts sentencing minor pot offenders to rehab in lieu of jail. According to state and national statistics, up to 70 percent of all individuals in drug treatment for marijuana are placed there by the criminal justice system. Of those in treatment, some 36 percent had not even used marijuana in the 30 days prior to their admission. These are the "addicts"?

Indeed, the concept of pot addiction is big business—even if the evidence in support of the pseudosyndrome is flimsy at best.

Studies Do Not Support Addiction Model

And what *does* the science say? Well, according to the nonpartisan National Academy of Sciences Institute of Medicine—which published a multiyear, million-dollar federal study assessing marijuana and health in 1999—"millions of Americans have tried marijuana, but most are not regular users [and] few marijuana users become dependent on it." The investigator added, "[A]though [some] marijuana users develop dependence, they appear to be less likely to do so than users of other drugs (including alcohol and nicotine), and marijuana dependence appears to be less severe than dependence on other drugs."

Cannabis withdrawal symptoms are typically limited to feelings of mild anxiety, irritability, agitation and insomnia.

Just how less likely? According to the Institute of Medicine's [IOM] 267-page report, fewer than 10 percent of those who try cannabis ever meet the clinical criteria for a diagnosis of "drug dependence". . . . By contrast, the IOM reported that 32 percent of tobacco users, 23 percent of heroin users, 17 percent of cocaine users and 15 percent of alcohol users meet the criteria for "drug dependence."

In short, it's the legal drugs that have Americans hooked—not pot.

Marijuana Withdrawal Symptoms Are Mild

But what about the claims that ceasing marijuana smoking can trigger withdrawal symptoms similar to those associated with quitting tobacco? Once again, it's a matter of degree. According to the Institute of Medicine, pot's withdrawal symptoms, when identified, are "mild and subtle" compared with the profound physical syndromes associated with ceasing chronic alcohol use—which can be fatal—or those abstinence symptoms associated with daily tobacco use, which are typically severe enough to persuade individuals to reinitiate their drug-taking behavior.

The IOM report further explained, "[U]nder normal cannabis use, the long half-life and slow elimination from the body of THC [tetrahydrocannabinol, the main psychoactive substance found in marijuana] prevent[s] substantial abstinence symptoms" from occurring. As a result, cannabis' withdrawal symptoms are typically limited to feelings of mild anxiety, irritability, agitation and insomnia.

Most importantly, unlike the withdrawal symptoms associated with the cessation of most other intoxicants, pot's mild after-effects do not appear to be either severe or long-lasting enough to perpetuate marijuana use in individuals who have decided to quit. This is why most marijuana smokers report voluntarily ceasing their cannabis use by age 30 with little physical or psychological difficulty. By comparison, many cigarette smokers who pick up the habit early in life continue to smoke for the rest of their lives, despite making numerous efforts to quit.

So let's review.

Marijuana is widely accepted by the National Academy of Sciences, the Canadian Senate Special Committee on Illegal Drugs, the British Advisory Council on the Misuse of Drugs and others to lack the severe physical and psychological dependence liability associated with most other intoxicants, including alcohol and tobacco. Further, pot lacks the profound abstinence symptoms associated with most legal intoxicants, including caffeine.

That's not to say that some marijuana smokers don't find quitting difficult. Naturally, a handful of folks do, though this subpopulation is hardly large enough to warrant pot's legal classification (along with heroin) as an illicit substance with a "high potential for abuse." Nor does this fact justify the continued arrest of more than 800,000 Americans annually for pot violations any more than such concerns would warrant the criminalization of booze or nicotine.

Now if I can only get NIDA to fork me over that $4 million check.

5

Marijuana Has Known Medical Benefits

The Economist

The Economist *is an English-language weekly news and international affairs publication edited in London.*

If marijuana had just been discovered it would be regarded as a medical breakthrough, but because of its history it is considered a dangerous, politically controversial drug. The U.S. Food and Drug Administration (FDA) denies that smoked marijuana has any accepted medical use in America, contradicting an earlier report by the Institute of Medicine as well as the experience of doctors and patients who find it helpful. The FDA approved Marinol, a synthetic version of one of the many active ingredients ("cannabinoids") in marijuana, but Marinol does not seem to work as well as marijuana itself, probably because many other cannabinoids interact in complex ways to produce a greater effect. More research would improve our ability to use marijuana medically, but the U.S. Drug Enforcement Administration's unwillingness to allow researchers to grow it makes such studies very difficult. Controversy with smoked marijuana may be avoided by other methods of administration, such as vaporization or an extract sprayed under the tongue. However, allowing researchers to breed varieties of marijuana is still necessary to learn more about which cannabinoids are having what effects. Such research is making great strides in other countries, which has resulted in a new marijuana treatment called Sativex being made available in Canada and elsewhere. Sativex is being studied for possible approval in the United States, but meanwhile the medical need for marijuana could be cheaply and easily met if the government had the will to do so.

Marijuana is medically useful, whether politicians like it or not.

If cannabis were unknown, and bioprospectors were suddenly to find it in some remote mountain crevice, its discovery would no doubt be hailed as a medical breakthrough. Scientists would praise its potential for treating everything from pain to cancer, and marvel at its rich pharmacopoeia—many of whose chemicals mimic vital molecules in the human body. In reality, cannabis has been with humanity for thousands of years and is considered by many governments (notably America's) to be a dangerous drug without utility. Any suggestion that the plant might be medically useful is politically controversial, whatever the science says. It is in this context that, on April 20th [2006], America's Food and Drug Administration (FDA) issued a statement saying that smoked marijuana has no accepted medical use in treatment in the United States.

Scientific Support for Medical Benefits of Marijuana

The statement is curious in a number of ways. For one thing, it overlooks a report made in 1999 by the Institute of Medicine (IOM), part of the National Academy of Sciences, which came to a different conclusion. John Benson, a professor of medicine at the University of Nebraska who co-chaired the committee that drew up the report, found some sound scientific information that supports the medical use of marijuana for certain patients for short periods—even for smoked marijuana.

This is important, because one of the objections to marijuana is that, when burned, its smoke contains many of the harmful things found in tobacco smoke, such as carcinogenic tar, cyanide and carbon monoxide. Yet the IOM report supports what some patients suffering from multiple sclerosis, AIDS and cancer—and their doctors—have known for a long time. This is that the drug gives them medicinal benefits over and above the medications they are already receiving, and despite the fact that the smoke has risks. That is probably why several studies show that many doctors recommend smoking cannabis to their patients, even though they are unable to prescribe it. Patients then turn to the black market for their supply.

Another reason the FDA statement is odd is that it seems to lack common sense. Cannabis has been used as a medicinal plant for millennia. In fact, the American government actually supplied cannabis as a medicine for some time, before the scheme was shut down in the early 1990s. Today, cannabis is used all over the world, despite its illegality, to relieve pain and anxiety, to aid sleep, and to prevent seizures and muscle spasms. For example, two of its long-advocated benefits are that it suppresses vomiting and enhances appetite—qualities that AIDS patients and those on anti-cancer chemotherapy find useful. So useful, in fact, that the FDA has licensed a drug called Marinol, a synthetic version of one of the active ingredients of marijuana—delta-9-tetrahydrocannabinol (THC). Unfortunately, many users of Marinol complain that it gets them high (which isn't what they actually want) and is not nearly as effective, nor cheap, as the real weed itself.

This may be because Marinol is ingested into the stomach, meaning that it is metabolised before being absorbed. Or it may be because the medicinal benefits of cannabis come from the synergistic effect of the multiplicity of chemicals it contains.

Just what have you been smoking?

THC is the best known active ingredient of cannabis, but by no means the only one. At the last count, marijuana was known to contain nearly 70 different cannabinoids, as THC and its cousins are collectively known. These chemicals activate receptor molecules in the human body, particularly the cannabinoid receptors on the surfaces of some nerve cells in the brain, and stimulate changes in biochemical activity. But the details often remain vague—in particular, the details of which molecules are having which clinical effects.

Today, cannabis is used all over the world . . . to relieve pain and anxiety, to aid sleep, and to prevent seizures and muscle spasms.

Political Barriers to Research

More clinical research would help. In particular, the breeding of different varieties of cannabis, with different mixtures of cannabinoids, would enable researchers to find out whether one variety works better for, say, multiple sclerosis-related spasticity while another works for AIDS-related nerve pain. However, in the United States, this kind of work has been inhibited by marijuana's illegality and the unwillingness of the Drug Enforcement Administration (DEA) to license researchers to grow it for research.

Since 2001, for example, Lyle Craker, a researcher at the University of Massachusetts, has been trying to obtain a licence from the DEA to grow cannabis for use in clinical research. After years of prevarication, and pressure on the DEA to make a decision, Dr Craker's application was turned down in 2004. Today, the saga continues and a DEA judge (who presides over a quasi-judicial process within the agency) is hearing an appeal, which could come to a close this summer. Dr Craker says that his situation is like that described in Joseph Heller's novel, "Catch 22". "We can say that this has no medical benefit because no tests have been done, and then we refuse to let you do any tests. The US has gotten into a bind, it has made cannabis out to be such a villain that people blindly say 'no.'"

The federal government has been rattled in recent years by the fact that eleven states have passed laws allowing the medical use of marijuana.

Anjuli Verma, the advocacy director of the American Civil Liberties Union (ACLU), a group helping Dr Craker fight his appeal, says that even if the DEA judge rules in their favour, the agency's chief administrator can still decide whether to allow the application. And, as she points out, the DEA is a political organisation charged with enforcing the drug laws. So, she says, the ACLU is in this for the long haul, and is already prepared for another appeal—one that would be heard in a federal court in the normal judicial system.

Ms Verma's view of the FDA's statement is that other arms of government are putting pressure on the agency to make a public pronouncement that conforms with drug ideology as promulgated by the White House, the DEA and a number of vocal anti-cannabis congressmen. In particular, the federal government has been rattled in recent years by the fact that eleven states have passed laws allowing the medical use of marijuana. In this context it is notable that the FDA's statement emphasises that it is smoked marijuana which has not gone through the process necessary to make it a prescription drug. (Nor would it be likely to, with all of the harmful things in the smoke.) The statement's emphasis on smoked marijuana is important because it leaves the door open for the agency to approve other methods of delivery.

Donald Abrams, a professor of clinical medicine at the University of California, San Francisco, has been working on one such option. He is allowed by the National Institute on

Drug Abuse (the only legal supplier of cannabis in the United States) to do research on a German nebuliser that heats cannabis to the point of vaporisation, where it releases its cannabinoids without any of the smoke of a spliff, and with fewer carcinogens.

That is encouraging. But it does not address the wider question of which cannabinoids are doing what. For that, researchers need to be able to do their own plant-breeding programmes.

Other Countries Are Doing the Needed Research

In America, this is impossible. But it is happening in other countries. In 1997, for example, the British government asked Geoffrey Guy, the executive chairman and founder of GW Pharmaceuticals, to come up with a programme to develop cannabis into a pharmaceutical product.

There is unmet medical need that . . . could easily and cheaply be met—if the American government cared more about suffering and less about posturing

---

In the intervening years, GW has assembled a "library" of more than 300 varieties of cannabis, and obtained plant-breeder's rights on between 30 and 40 of these. It has found the genes that control cannabinoid production and can specify within strict limits the seven or eight cannabinoids it is most interested in. And it knows how to crossbreed its strains to get the mixtures it wants.

Nor is this knowledge merely academic. Last year, GW gained approval in Canada for the use of its first drug, Sativex, which is an extract of cannabis sprayed under the tongue that is designed for the relief of neuropathic pain in multiple sclerosis. Sativex is also available to a more limited degree in

Spain and Britain, and is in clinical trials for other uses, such as relieving the pain of rheumatoid arthritis.

At the start of [2006], the company made the first step towards gaining regulatory approval for Sativex in America when the FDA accepted it as a legitimate candidate for clinical trials. But there is still a long way to go.

And that delay raises an important point. Once available, a well-formulated and scientifically tested drug should knock a herbal medicine into a cocked hat. No one would argue for chewing willow bark when aspirin is available. But, in the meantime, there is unmet medical need that, as the IOM report pointed out, could easily and cheaply be met—if the American government cared more about suffering and less about posturing.

6

Medical Marijuana Lacks Scientific Support

Peter J. Cohen

Peter J. Cohen is an adjunct professor of law at Georgetown University.

In 2004, the Supreme Court ruled in Ashcroft vs. Raich *that the U.S. Drug Enforcement Administration could enforce federal drug laws against two individuals who were legally growing medical marijuana according to the Compassionate Use Act in California [Proposition 215]. The* Raich *ruling ignored the more important implication of Proposition 215, that a medical treatment could be approved by popular vote rather than by proper scientific evaluation. Based on anecdotal evidence of marijuana's medical use both currently and historically, advocates of medical marijuana claim it is an effective pharmacological treatment, yet wish to exempt it from the evaluation by the U.S. Food and Drug Administration (FDA) that any other drug treatment must undergo. If it had successfully gone through the evaluation process it could now be legitimately used as a medicine, as are many other plant-based "controlled substances." Despite the FDA's approval of Marinol, which contains the principal psychoactive ingredient of marijuana, the plant contains other substances which may have beneficial effects, and more and better studies are required. The Food, Drug, and Cosmetic Act requires that drugs not be advertised and sold unless they have gone through very rigorous scientific investigations, and the need for such research is not invalidated by political barriers making such research difficult to conduct. Smoked marijuana should not get an easy path to drug approval, because people need to be protected from the false hope of unproven medicines.*

A [2005] article in the *Hastings Center Report* reviewed the Supreme Court's current (but undoubtedly not final) delineation of the boundaries of federal power as set forth by the Constitution's commerce clause. The question before the Court [in the 2004 case *Ashcroft vs. Raich*] was straightforward: Did federal authority asserted under the Controlled Substance Act of 1970 (CSA) trump California's legalization of "medical marijuana" when these plants were grown within the state and were not bought, sold, or transported into another state? By a six to three vote, the *Raich* court held that the federal Drug Enforcement Administration could enforce the CSA against two individuals who were growing marijuana for their own medical use in full compliance with California's Compassionate Use Act (Proposition 215). At the same time, the Court's holding neither struck down Proposition 215 nor demanded that California bring criminal charges against its citizens who were using marijuana on the advice of their physicians.

Medical Marijuana Policy Should Not Be Decided By Popular Vote

Unfortunately, the far more significant policy question raised by Proposition 215 was never adjudicated. In effect, Proposition 215 declared that some compounds used to treat disease could be evaluated and approved by a vote of the people rather than "by experts qualified by scientific training and experience," as mandated by the Food, Drug, and Cosmetic Act. But Proposition 215 was wrong as a matter of public policy. Anecdotes, Internet blogs, and advertisements do not provide a sound basis for assessing the safety and efficacy of pharmacologic agents. "Medical marijuana" should be subjected to the same scientific scrutiny as any drug proposed for use in medical therapy, rather than made legal for medical use by popular will.

In *Raich* and other cases involving Proposition 215, marijuana's advocates presented this compound to the courts as a drug, a pharmaceutical agent efficacious in the treatment of serious and even life-threatening illnesses [Evelyn Nieves, in a June 7, 2005, *Washington Post* article, wrote,]:

> Indeed, for Raich, 39, a mother of two teenagers who says she has been suffering from a litany of disabling ailments since she was a teenager herself, medical cannabis has worked where scores of other prescribed drugs have failed. . . . It relieves pain, she said, from progressive scoliosis, endometriosis and tumors in her uterus. Raich even believes it has something to do with arresting the growth of an inoperable brain tumor.
>
> She is convinced that her use of medical marijuana, which began in 1997 after she had been using a wheelchair for two years, made her strong enough to stand up and learn to walk again. She said doctors could find no other explanation.

These extravagant claims notwithstanding, marijuana has been used as a therapeutic agent throughout history, as Mathew W. Grey noted in a 1996 review of the use of medical marijuana:

> Cannabis, more commonly referred to as marijuana, has a long history of medical use in this country and worldwide. Accounts dating back as far as 2700 B.C. describe the Chinese using marijuana for maladies ranging from rheumatism to constipation. There are similar reports of Indians, Africans, ancient Greeks and medieval Europeans using the substance to treat fevers, dysentery and malaria. In the United States, physicians documented the therapeutic properties of the drug as early as 1840, and the drug was included in the United States Pharmacopoeia, the official list

of recognized medical drugs, from 1850 through 1942. During this period, lack of appetite was one of the indications for marijuana prescription.

In order to evaluate various hypotheses concerning the potential utility of marijuana in various therapeutic areas, more and better studies would be needed.

Classifying Medical Marijuana as a Drug

Such anecdotal reports have been used by marijuana's adherents to support their wish to exempt the drug from the same scrutiny required for any other compound that is used to treat, ameliorate, or prevent human disease. Specifically, they have never campaigned vigorously for medical marijuana's evaluation by the Food and Drug Administration [FDA]. Had those who favored the use of smoked marijuana as a drug elected not to circumvent the Food, Drug, and Cosmetic Act, and had smoked marijuana successfully traversed the same FDA regulatory process required for any drug proposed for use in medical treatment, it would have attained the status of an approved pharmaceutical. It could then have been purchased legally and used for medical purposes when prescribed by a properly licensed physician.

Why should FDA approval have been sought? Why should "medical marijuana" have been classified as a drug rather than a botanical, an herbal medication, or a folk remedy? The answer is in the Food, Drug, and Cosmetic Act itself: "The term 'drug' means articles intended for use in the diagnosis, cure, mitigation, treatment, or prevention of disease in man . . . and articles (other than food) intended to affect the structure or any function of the body of man." That smoked marijuana is both a "controlled substance" and a plant product is extraneous to this discussion. Controlled substances have widespread use in legitimate medical practice. As an anesthesiologist, I have legally administered more narcotics (in the course of

51

providing medical care) than many low-level illegal drug dealers. Plants and their derivatives can be potent medications.
During my internship, I used digitalis leaf (derived from the
foxglove plant) to treat congestive heart failure. Botanicals are
the active ingredients in tincture of opium and belladonna
suppositories, both of which are legal and FDA-approved
when employed for legitimate therapeutic use. Smoked marijuana could achieve the same status were the FDA to find it
safe and effective for medical use.

---

*Until studies are done using scientifically acceptable clini-
cal trial design and subjected to appropriate statistical
analysis, the questions concerning the therapeutic utility
of marijuana will likely remain largely unanswered.*

Accurate, Unbiased Research Is Needed

A Consensus Conference convened by the National Institutes
of Health [NIH] on February 19–20, 1997, to discuss the role
of legitimate scientific research in evaluating the safety and efficacy of smoked marijuana reiterated the need for accurate
and nonbiased scientific investigation of medical marijuana.
The final report from the conference acknowledged that the
FDA has approved a drug known as Marinol, which contains
tetrahydrocannabinol (THC, the active psychotropic ingredient of *Cannabis sativa*, and a controlled substance), for oral
use in treating both loss of appetite due to the AIDS-wasting
syndrome and chemotherapy-induced nausea and vomiting,
but then offered a caution:

> [This] does not fully satisfy the need to evaluate the poten-
> tial medical utility of marijuana. The Expert Group noted
> that, although [THC] is the principal psychoactive compo-
> nent of the cannabis leaf, there may be other compounds in
> the leaf that have useful therapeutic properties. Further-
> more, the bioavailability and pharmacokinetics [the process

by which a drug is absorbed, metabolized, and eliminated by the body] of THC from smoked marijuana are substantially different than those of the oral dosage form.

The Consensus Conference also observed that other pharmacologic agents had already been approved to treat many of the disorders for which marijuana's claims had not been scientifically substantiated. Yet, the report stated, "this does not mean, however, that the issue should be foreclosed. It simply means that in order to evaluate various hypotheses concerning the potential utility of marijuana in various therapeutic areas, more and better studies would be needed."

Finally, the consultants felt that the evidence to date showed medical marijuana might have a significant role in the areas of appetite stimulation and cachexia (bodily wasting in the late stages of cancer), nausea and vomiting following anticancer therapy, neurological and movement disorders, analgesia, and glaucoma. At the same time, they made it clear that these possibilities would never reach fruition in the absence of scientific data:

> Until studies are done using scientifically acceptable clinical trial design and subjected to appropriate statistical analysis, the questions concerning the therapeutic utility of marijuana will likely remain much as they have to date—largely unanswered. To the extent that the NIH can facilitate the development of a scientifically rigorous and relevant database, the NIH should do so.

Political barriers to the performance of scientifically valid studies of medical marijuana do not obviate the argument that marijuana should be assessed in the same way as other drugs proposed for therapy.

Political Barriers to Research

The Food, Drug, and Cosmetic Act requires that drugs may not be advertised and sold in the absence of "evidence consisting of adequate and well-controlled investigations, including clinical investigations, by experts qualified by scientific training and experience to evaluate the effectiveness of the drug involved." However, the road to approval is not easy, and many investigators attempting to carry out scientific studies of marijuana have encountered political obstacles. Consider, for example, the difficulties faced by Donald Abrams, Professor of Medicine at the University of California, San Francisco, and chair of the Bay Area's Community Consortium on HIV research, in his attempts to study the effects of smoked marijuana on AIDS wasting. Abrams, a clinical pharmacologist, had proposed a study to provide objective data on whether smoked marijuana could ease the symptoms of AIDS wasting and produce gains in body weight. His university's institutional review board had approved the study, the FDA had approved it, and the university planned to fund it. Nonetheless, his request to import marijuana from the Netherlands was rejected.

Smoked marijuana ought not to be allowed to take the easy path to drug approval.

Since the National Institute on Drug Abuse (NIDA) grows marijuana that is supplied to appropriate scientific investigators, the professor requested their assistance. However, because his funding had originated at his university, and not the NIH, of which NIDA is a part, he was denied access to the product. The NIH stated that its policy was to make marijuana available only to investigators who had received a peer-reviewed NIH grant to conduct the proposed study.

In May of 1996, Dr. Abrams resubmitted his study proposal to the National Institute of Health, believing that he had addressed NIDA's concerns. At that time, the study was still approved and funded at the university level. In October 1996, four years after he had initiated requests to obtain marijuana legally, he was again informed that NIH's Mississippi marijuana "farm" would not supply the needed cannabis. . . . The following month, the people of California voters passed Proposition 215 by a wide margin.

People Need to Be Protected from Unproven Therapies

Political barriers to the performance of scientifically valid studies of medical marijuana do not obviate the argument that marijuana should be assessed in the same way as other drugs proposed for therapy. The sick still need medically sound treatments. In the case of Angel Raich, unfortunately, scientific evidence of this drug's efficacy in curing her inoperable brain tumor is simply nonexistent.

Decades ago, the Supreme Court [in the 1979 case *United States vs. Rutherford*] gave an ample argument for protecting people from the vain hope of unproven therapy:

> Since the turn of the century, resourceful entrepreneurs have advertised a wide variety of purportedly simple and painless cures for cancer, including liniments of turpentine, mustard, oil, eggs, and ammonia; peat moss; arrangements of colored flood-lamps; pastes made from glycerine and limburger cheese. . . . In citing these examples, we do not, of course, intend to deprecate the sincerity of Laetrile's [an ineffective and toxic plant-based medicine] current proponents, or to imply any opinion on whether that drug may ultimately prove safe and effective for cancer treatment. But this historical experience does suggest why Congress could reasonably have determined to protect the terminally ill, no less than other patients, from the vast range of self-styled panaceas that inventive minds can devise.

Smoked marijuana ought not to be allowed to take the easy path to drug approval. Marinol, containing pure THC, has already been approved in the United States. Sativex, another formulation of THC, has been approved in Canada and is under consideration in the United States. Smoked marijuana might also be approved and legally prescribed for appropriate therapeutic uses.

I cannot resist a final thought. Had *Cannabis sativa* not been proscribed by the Controlled Substances Act (and been taxed and regulated, as are alcohol and tobacco, two substances that cause far more "societal pathology"), every "medical marijuana" case would have been moot. And under this scenario, as long as smoked marijuana was not advertised as an FDA-approved pharmaceutical (which would hardly have been necessary), it would undoubtedly have become one of this century's premier herbal medications.

Marijuana Use Is Unhealthy

E.J. Sanna

In addition to being an author and a journalist, E.J. Sanna has a background in chemistry.

Users of marijuana may experience many different effects, including some very unpleasant ones. The American Psychiatric Association recognizes a number of marijuana-caused mental disorders, which may last for long periods of time. Smoking marijuana disrupts the immune system, puts users at greater risk of developing lung cancer than that faced by tobacco smokers, can cause emphysema and other lung diseases, and increases the risk of heart attack. Brain function is adversely affected and connections have been found between marijuana use and bipolar disorder, schizophrenia, and other mental problems—including the ability to learn and cope with everyday responsibilities. The drug can adversely affect the reproductive system and harm unborn babies. Driving skills are impaired long after the user's euphoria has worn off. Marijuana can be physically and emotionally addictive, and its use often precedes the use of heavier drugs.

[A] teen tells his story on the Marijuana Anonymous Web site:

> *The first time I smoked weed was during the summer before eighth grade. I was really curious to see what it was all about. I had a few hits, but didn't really get stoned. Later, I smoked some more. I got so high I didn't even know what was going*

on. The next chance I got to get high, I jumped on it. The more I did it, the more I liked it. I loved the way pot played with my head.

Finally, I got caught. I was grounded for a while, but I went right back to it. That happened over and over until my parents decided to put me in a chemical dependency program. I managed to still smoke pot on the day furthest from my drug tests. I tried all those purification concoctions, but my dad eventually found out. I was still determined not to let anybody rob me of my "God-given rights," so I continued to smoke bud and got "dirty" drug tests. My grades weren't really suffering so I saw no reason to stop. I kept getting into more trouble.

Finally, disaster struck. I was caught at school. My hearing to determine whether I am expelled or not happens very soon. My eyes have been opened. Getting caught once can ruin your life. By staying sober, I am getting all my privileges back. As for school, I hope to be allowed back in. My only job is to stay out of trouble.

Marijuana Effects Vary

The way that a person feels or reacts after taking marijuana can be decided by many factors. Not all people will have noticeable adverse effects, nor will everyone be able to escape with only a pleasant high. How a user reacts to cannabis can be affected by how many times a person has previously used the same drug, how much THC [delta-9-tetrahydrocannabinol, the main psychoactive ingredient in marijuana] is present in the marijuana, how the drug is consumed, and whether or not the marijuana is mixed with other drugs or alcohol. Things like the user's expectations and where the drug is used can change how a person reacts as well.

There are many possible responses to a drug like marijuana. Some people may feel nothing at all after taking the drug. Others will feel a high—relaxed and happy. At other times, the marijuana results in physical feelings of hunger or thirst, often known as the "munchies." However, there are more adverse effects as well. Anxiety attacks and paranoia often accompany marijuana use, especially when it contains a lot of THC. One thing is sure, sooner or later all marijuana users suffer from some kind of unwanted side effect after using the drug. While some of these are short term and will go away after the THC is out of the person's system, some are more long term and can cause permanent damage to a user's body.

Marijuana kills helpful cells like macrophages and T-cells, which are responsible for fighting off germs in the body.

Marijuana can cause disruptions in perception, memory, and judgment. While these go away in time, especially when they occur in first-time users, they can last for at least six weeks after the drug is used. These cannabis-caused mental disorders are accepted as real diseases and have their own category in the *Diagnostic and Statistical Manual of Mental Disorders*, which is published by the American Psychiatric Association. These impairments include "cannabis intoxication," which is characterized by a loss of motor coordination, anxiety, a loss of judgment, withdrawal, and sometimes hallucinations. "Cannabis intoxication delirium" is another disorder; this one consists of a loss of memory and disorientation.

There are short-term physical effects to marijuana as well, including a raised heartbeat, bloodshot eyes, and/or dry mouth. These effects, as well as other, mental results of using the drug, can be magnified if any other drug is used at the same time. While all these side effects may sound bad enough, other more serious long-term consequences can occur as well.

Disruption of the Immune System

Smoking marijuana daily can lead to many adverse outcomes, especially where the immune system is concerned. Cells in the bronchial passages protect the body against any bacteria or other microorganisms that may be inhaled. Marijuana kills these cells, meaning that germs are more likely to get into a person's body and cause damage. Cannabis also reduces the body's ability to fight off harmful diseases. This means that people are more likely to die from an otherwise treatable disease, like pneumonia, which often proves fatal in people with weakened immune systems.

Marijuana kills helpful cells like macrophages and T-cells, which are responsible for fighting off germs in the body. When these are gone, diseases can overcome a person easily. Studies have shown that marijuana use may cause HIV patients to develop AIDS. The body is not only unable to fight against diseases like AIDS or cancer, but it is more susceptible to these and other diseases. While marijuana does not cause death in these cases, fatality is a very possible result; when people's immune systems are weakened by the drug, many diseases that would be easily fought off by a normal person can prove dangerous.

Marijuana users are putting themselves at an even greater risk of developing cancer than tobacco users are.

Effects on Heart and Lungs

A study that compared 173 people with cancer to 176 healthy people showed that smoking marijuana increases the chance of getting cancer in the head or neck. The more marijuana that was smoked, the higher the likelihood was.

When most people think of lung cancer, they think of cigarette smoke. However, marijuana can cause the same results, since both kinds of smoke contain many of the same toxic chemicals, including those known to cause cancer. Marijuana may even be more of a cancer threat than tobacco, since it contains four times the amount of tar that one regular cigarette does. The marijuana smoke also contains 50 to 75 percent more than tobacco smoke of the hydrocarbons that are proven to be carcinogenic. An enzyme that is present in marijuana smoke, which converts hydrocarbons to forms that can cause cancer, increases this effect. When you add this to the fact that people smoking a joint are more likely to hold the smoke in longer and breath it in deeper than tobacco users are, marijuana users are putting themselves at an even greater risk of developing cancer than tobacco users are.

Lung cancer is not the only adverse effect from marijuana on the respiratory system. Diseases like emphysema, chronic bronchitis, and respiratory tract infections also happen as a result of the inhalation of marijuana smoke. The toxins in the drug cause the air passages in the lungs to close up so they don't work as well, and the lungs to become inflamed.

A study of a group of 450 people found that those who use marijuana frequently have more health problems, especially involving their respiratory tract. These individuals felt sick more and missed more days of work than those who didn't smoke. This is not surprising when one considers that even occasional users frequently have burning and stinging in their mouths, as well as heavy coughs.

Because of the depression and anxiety that results from marijuana use, the drug can cause disruptions in daily life.

Studies have shown that the chance of a heart attack goes up by more than four times in the first hour after someone smokes marijuana. While scientists are not sure why this occurs, they think it may be because marijuana use increases blood pressure and heart rate. It also causes the blood to lose some of its ability to carry oxygen, making the heart work harder. All these factors lead to the ideal conditions for a heart attack.

A Decrease in Mental Health

While marijuana can cause many problems to various body organs, the brain is also adversely affected. Studies have indicated a connection between marijuana and mental disorders like panic attacks, flashbacks, delusions, paranoia, and hallucinations. Marijuana has also been known to cause flare-ups in people who already have mental illnesses like bipolar disorder and schizophrenia.

Even first-time users can suffer from these results. Between 10 and 15 percent of people who smoked marijuana said that they felt confused or paranoid after using the drug and cited these as disadvantages of using cannabis. Twenty-seven percent said these feelings occurred regularly. This is caused by the binding of THC to the various brain cells many located in the areas of the brain that control memory, thought, and concentration.

Another result of long-term marijuana use is a change in the nerve cells that contain and produce dopamine. Dopamine regulates the feelings of motivation and the rewards we give ourselves for various behaviors. Marijuana is just one of many drugs that affects this chemical.

Because of the depression and anxiety that results from marijuana use, the drug can cause disruptions in daily life. People who use marijuana regularly are more likely to have trouble learning new skills or remembering information, making them fall behind in work or their everyday responsibilities. The good news is that these memory losses may not be permanent. Researchers recently tested a group of heavy marijuana smokers on their ability to remember words from a list. They were impaired while using the drug and for a week after quitting, but after about four weeks, their memories returned to normal.

Students have an especially hard time coping with marijuana use. Teens who use pot are less likely to graduate; they get lower grades in class and on standardized tests. While two people may score equally well on tests in fourth grade, by the time both are seniors, the marijuana smoker will score significantly lower.

Effects on the Reproduction System

Like many drugs, marijuana can lead to problems with the reproduction system. Both men and women have reported a temporary loss of fertility after using marijuana. The drug also has adverse effects on unborn babies. Some research has indicated that the use of marijuana during pregnancy can lead to miscarriages. Babies who are born to mothers who are marijuana users are often born prematurely or with low birth weights.

Children born to mothers who were frequent marijuana users were shown to be more nervous and apt to cry, as well as having a different response to visual stimuli than most infants that age. While this doesn't prove anything on its own, it may point to neurological defects. This conclusion is reinforced by the fact that between the ages of infancy and preschool, these children are more likely to have behavioral issues and a poorer performance in school as they continue to grow.

Driving Under the Influence

As already stated, marijuana influences skills like coordination, the ability to concentrate, and reaction time. While this is never good, it can be especially dangerous when a person is driving. People under the influence of cannabis, as with other drugs or alcohol, have a hard time responding to signals on the road in time to avoid an accident. These necessary skills are impaired for at least four to six hours after using one joint, long after the user has lost the euphoria of a high.

Studies of patients in shock-trauma units because of car accidents have shown that about 15 percent of those who had been driving a car or motorcycle when they crashed had been under the influence of marijuana. When reckless drivers were tested at the scene for drugs, more than 33 percent tested positive for marijuana; 12 percent were positive for both pot and cocaine.

Cannabis can be both physically and emotionally addictive.

Marijuana: An Addictive Drug

Long-term marijuana use often leads to addiction. People start craving the drug—they are unable to function without it. More than 150,000 people each year get treatment for their marijuana addictions, which are characterized by an uncontrollable urge for the drug. Cannabis addicts use the drug even when they know that the drug is not in their best interests. Symptoms of marijuana addiction include:

- a tolerance for the drug

- the inability to cut down or control marijuana use

- the use of a huge amount of time to smoke marijuana

- a decrease in social activities because of marijuana use

- continued use, even though it is causing the individual problems

Cannabis can be both physically and emotionally addictive. Abusers define themselves by the drug. They are always thinking about it and when they will next get high. They think of marijuana as a miracle cure for all their problems.

When these people do try to quit, they often find that they can't. They may experience irritability, insomnia, and anxiety when they attempt to stop using marijuana. These are all signs of withdrawal; the body is now dependent on the drug and finds it hard to survive without it. Withdrawal is also characterized by tension and decreases in appetite. While symptoms appear within twenty-four hours of the last dose of cannabis, they can last up to twenty-eight days.

Other Effects

Marijuana stays in the body long after the drug is consumed. The body, especially the fat, absorbs THC, and it is transformed into metabolites in an attempt for the body to rid itself of the foreign substance. These metabolites can be present in urine tests for up to a week after use.

Another problem is that marijuana is often considered a gateway drug, a drug that leads to other, heavier drugs. While this is not technically proven, it has been shown that very few adolescents use other illicit drugs without trying marijuana first. Part of this is because marijuana is relatively easy to obtain, and use puts people in contact with people who can buy and sell other drugs as well. After teens learn how to buy marijuana, they can also easily get hold of other substances.

Clearly, marijuana use has serious consequences. Physical and mental side effects are only one side of the story. Marijuana use has legal and social ramifications as well.

8

Marijuana Can Help Ease Chronic Pain

Jana Christian

Jana Christian is a contributor to Lester Grinspoon's Marijuana Uses Web site, which publishes reports from people who have benefited from the use of marijuana.

The author and her husband suffer from chronic pain and have found that marijuana is the only medicine that relieves their symptoms. When medical marijuana is unavailable, the quality of their lives deteriorates greatly. In their experience, marijuana has many beneficial properties, including pain relief, muscle relaxation, and enhancement of creativity. Without marijuana these chronic pain sufferers barely feel human, experiencing sleeplessness, sorrow, suffering, and even the risk of suicide. The author ends with an impassioned plea for help in legalizing medical marijuana.

I'm a 57-year-old woman disabled through chronic pain. My husband and I live with identical injuries in our necks and lumbar spines and, as a result, Chronic Pain from Hell.

My husband and I were just discussing marijuana again, a subject near and dear to both of our hearts. Recently we just existed for over a week with NO marijuana. As we use it for Chronic Pain, a week and a half is an eternity to people like us.

We've both noticed there's a pattern for us. We start trying to talk ourselves into the fact that it's okay to be out of pot,

Jana Christian, "Chronic Pain from Hell," Dr. Lester Grinspoon's Marijuana Uses, November 20, 2008. Reproduced by permission.

that we'll be fine. Maybe we'll even give it up and save money. But it's all that we use for pain relief. We start sniping a little at each other. In the past, we would substitute alcohol. Alcohol may cut us off from the pain momentarily, but we will be at each other's throats in a matter of hours, there's just no question. And that exacerbates stress, and stress begets more pain through clenching of bodies in response to the stress.

Marijuana's Beneficial Properties

I've decided that the properties of marijuana have not been touted nearly enough, because how do you put such things into words? I'm a writer, but words to describe the feeling of having marijuana under our roof when we live in so much pain just have not been invented yet. That's how strongly we feel about it. But let me feebly attempt to try.

The truth about marijuana is this: It DOES allow a person who withdraws from life through pain to live a daily existence with some dignity.

Pot is the best muscle relaxer known to man. Everything relaxes. With agony like ours (nerve/spine pain), the perfect antidote for clenching your body clearly is marijuana. I watch my husband's facial muscles relax. He becomes a completely different person, someone I love to be around. I see him want to stretch his muscles, where prior to smoking marijuana, just ain't happening. He's lucky to shuffle across the room to some new position. I see his smile re-appear after long droughts of pot.

He gets involved with people and things he used to care about. He gets creative, I mean REALLY creative. His lyrics could rival Bob Dylan, he's THAT good. His food could blow Emeril's away. And his photography. . .never seen any better. Our minds are expanded to such a degree and that gives us a good day. We constantly smile, though we're still in the midst of pain. Just to feel human for ANY length of time is a blessing I just can't quite describe. Sometimes you'll notice you haven't had any pain for say, like, an hour. You scream "hallelujah" as if it's a National holiday. It's that noticeable.

Time away from our pain killer of choice is cause for much depression, and not because we're in withdrawal from marijuana's effects. It's because we start clenching our bodies again against every wave of pain. Our muscles get frozen in nasty positions. We are again UNABLE TO SLEEP. And IF you are lucky enough to sleep without the aid of pot, the fact that your neck remains in any position for too long means you're screwed when you do wake up. You know the two worst times of the day are when you wake up and when you go to bed. Both are agony.

So you go into mini-hock because the Feds tell you that what you choose for pain is illegal. Where is the research on that? And you can't buy that new bed you need desperately for relief, because your pain medicine (marijuana) is so expensive, you have to choose. And maybe IF you had medical insurance besides Medicare you would have to give in to the conventional and harmful medications of choice, narcotics, but in your heart, you know that your particular brain chemistry responds well and BEST to pot. But no one believes your story. You start to envision yourself in a lunasylum. Because you know your pain is so real it's SURREAL, yet your medication is illegal. But you need your medication, or suicide is sure to follow. (I know the three S's of Chronic Pain: sleeplessness, sorrow and suffering. I now add suicide, unless an intervention is made.)

And you live like second-class citizens because the powers that be don't bother to get to know herb. Well, I'm here to shout about it.

The Truth About Marijuana

The truth about marijuana is this: It DOES allow a person who withdraws from life through pain to live a daily existence with some dignity (quality of life, HELL; I'd settle for existence at this point). It allows the person dying from auto-immune disorders and body-decaying cancer to at least enjoy their last days eating the foods they once loved with an appetite produced by you-guessed-it, smoking marijuana.

It brings out long-suppressed creativity. Creativity once stunted maybe by coming from dysfunctional families who expressed NOTHING. Creativity stuffed further down by the shame of coming from these hideous places by picking up any animate object that momentarily changed who you were (but that was at least SOMEthing to feel—anything different from who you truly were). I started to empathize with people who cut themselves to release the emotional pain. And what a relief that could be. Marijuana has served as a sort of truth serum for me. It has allowed me to relax to the point of being me. And not hiding behind masks. And that's a lot.

All I wish is for someone to hear me, someone who can direct us to pain relief once and for all. Someone who can direct me to the person with the most influence RE: legalizing medical marijuana. I will continue to write my senators and congresswomen.

I pray that 2004 is a year to remember RE: getting something done about this drug UN-war. It frightens me more than I can say. Maybe I can make a difference.

9

Nonmedical Marijuana Use Is Extremely Risky

Joseph A. Califano Jr.

Joseph A. Califano Jr. is chairman and president of the National Center on Addiction and Substance Abuse at Columbia University.

Popular efforts to decriminalize marijuana for medical purposes have politicized what should be a scientific process. If ingredients of marijuana have healing properties, the U.S. Food and Drug Administration can approve them for medical use. Nonmedical use of marijuana carries significant risks that everyone who cares about children should know. The potency of marijuana increased enormously from 1992 to 2006, accompanied by a vast increase in cases of marijuana dependence. Large numbers of teens use marijuana, which interferes with driving skills and learning ability, as well as being linked to a variety of physical and mental health problems. Just as parents already protect children and teens from known dangers in many ways, they need to be aware of new scientific findings about the increased potency and dangers of marijuana today and take steps to prevent their children from using it. While parents are the most powerful prevention resource available, everyone who works with children and teens need to help detect marijuana use, intervene as necessary, and educate the country about the dangers of teen marijuana use. Law enforcement resources also should be used; when kids are

Joseph A. Califano Jr., "Accompanying Statement of Joseph A. Califano Jr. on Non-Medical Marijuana III: Rite of Passage or Russian Roulette?" National Center on Addiction and Substance Abuse at Columbia University, November 20, 2008. Reproduced by permission.

caught in marijuana-related crimes, they should be tested for drug use and other psychological problems, and given help if needed.

In 1999, CASA [National Center on Addiction and Substance Abuse] published its first White Paper [an authoritative report on a problem and how to solve it] on non-medical marijuana. *Non-Medical Marijuana: Rite of Passage or Russian Roulette?*, spelling out the implications of legalization for children. In 2004, CASA issued its second White Paper on the subject, alerting parents to findings about the relationship between marijuana use and the increased risk of using other drugs. This White Paper, *Non-Medical Marijuana III: Rite of Passage or Russian Roulette?*, third in the series, is prompted by the alarming increases in the potency of marijuana, and in teen emergency department mentions, treatment admissions and clinical diagnoses of marijuana abuse and dependence.

From 1992 to 2006, the potency of marijuana increased by 175.0 percent.

All these reports focus on non-medical marijuana. Searching for the therapeutic potential of cannabis and addressing issues related to efficacy, safety, benefits and risks are appropriate. These are, however, matters for doctors, scientists, the National Institutes of Health [NIH], the Food and Drug Administration [FDA] and pharmaceutical manufacturers rather than for public referenda. Efforts to decriminalize marijuana for medicinal purposes through popular referenda have politicized what should be a scientific process. To the extent that ingredients in marijuana possess properties that can efficaciously and safely relieve individuals suffering from AIDS or chemotherapy-related nausea, multiple sclerosis, or other ailments, the Food and Drug Administration can approve them for medical use.

Alarming Findings About Teen Marijuana Use

We have written this report about non-medical marijuana to alert parents, teachers, doctors, clergy and all those who care about our nation's children, to critical and alarming findings about teen marijuana use:

- From 1992 to 2006, the potency of marijuana increased by 175.0 percent.

- From 1992 to 2006, there has been a 492.1 percent increase in the proportion of treatment admissions for persons under age 18 where clinical (DSM) [*Diagnostic and Statistical Manual of Mental Disorders*] diagnosis was reported for marijuana abuse or dependence, compared with a 53.7 percent *decline* in the proportion of DSM diagnoses for all other substances of abuse (includes alcohol, illicit, controlled prescription and over-the-counter drugs, and inhalants).

- From 1992 to 2006, there has been a 188.1 percent increase in the proportion of treatment admissions for persons under age 18 who cite marijuana as their primary drug of abuse, compared with a 54.4 percent *decline* in the proportion of admissions for all other substances of abuse. This increase is driven, in part, by an increase in criminal justice referrals for treatment.

- From 1995 to 2002, the percentage of drug-related emergency department findings for marijuana as a major substance of abuse among 12- to 17-year-olds increased by 136.4 percent, more than five times the increase in findings for all other major substances of abuse (25.7 percent). [Consistent estimates for trends are available only for the period from 1995–2002.]

- Many teens are using marijuana more intensely than in the past. Rates of daily marijuana use among 12th graders tripled from 1992 to 1999 and have stubbornly resisted significant change since then. In 2007, approximately 204,000 high school seniors (5.1 percent) used marijuana on a daily basis.

- Despite recent declines in teen marijuana use, in 2007 the percentage of teens who had ever used marijuana was 26.8 percent higher among 8th graders, 44.9 percent higher among 10th graders and 28.2 percent higher among 12th graders than lows in 1992. By 2007, a total of 10.7 million 9th to 12th graders had used marijuana.

- Marijuana is the second most frequently detected psychoactive substance among drivers (alcohol is the first) and is associated with impaired driving skills. It is associated more strongly with juvenile crime than alcohol use and is linked to poor academic performance.

- Marijuana use interferes with brain functions such as memory, learning and attention, can damage the lungs and heart and increase the risk of other drug use, and has been linked to other mental health problems in young people, such as depression, anxiety and conduct disorders.

- Recent research suggests possible associations between marijuana use and schizophrenia and other psychotic disorders.

Marijuana Is More Dangerous Than Ever Before

The good news is that in recent years teen marijuana use and the percent of all teens who meet clinical criteria for marijuana abuse and dependence have declined. The bad news is that 10.7 million teens still report that they have used marijuana. The worst news is that for those who do use the drug there is growing cause for grave concern. The striking and parallel increases in marijuana's potency, in teen admissions to treatment for marijuana and in their diagnoses of marijuana abuse and dependence, and increases in emergency room findings linked to marijuana use together sound an alarm for parents and teens across the country. While not all teens who use marijuana will become addicted, experimentation is the first step to regular use. Regular marijuana use is a dangerous game of Russian roulette with the bullets of other drug use, addiction, interference with brain functioning, accidents, crime and health and social problems in the chamber.

Growing recognition of the dangers of marijuana use among teens has led Dr. Nora Volkow, Director of the National Institute on Drug Abuse, to state that "It is important to remind young people, their parents and others that marijuana is not a benign drug. Marijuana can be addictive; it interferes with critical brain functions, like learning and memory. And it may pose a threat to the health and well-being of children and adolescents at a critical point in their lives—when they are growing, learning, maturing, and laying the foundation for their adult years."

Marijuana can be an addictive drug with enormous health and social consequences.

The message for teens is clear: today's pernicious pot is not your parents' pot. The average THC [delta-9-tetrahydrocannabinoly the main psychoactive ingredient in marijuana] levels in seized marijuana samples in the mid-1970s were less than one percent compared to 8.8 percent today. According to Florida's Attorney General, "The increase in the drug's potency also has caused marijuana's market value to skyrocket. Hydroponic marijuana in some areas actually trades ounce for ounce with cocaine."

Children Must Be Protected from Marijuana

Just as society came to understand the dangers of tobacco use and parents took action to protect their children and teens, it is now time to face the facts about marijuana use. Marijuana can be an addictive drug with enormous health and social consequences. Teens have easy access to the drug and begin use at early ages; the earlier they begin, the greater the likelihood that they will use other drugs and become dependent. It is of critical importance that parents take action to prevent marijuana use among their children and to help them stop using if they have already begun.

Parents take extraordinary efforts to protect their children and teens from known dangers. We make sure that toys, playgrounds and cribs are safe. We avoid exposure to lead paint. We vaccinate our children against disease. We equip our children with safety helmets to wear when rollerblading, skateboarding or riding their bikes. We make sure that our children and teens buckle up when they get in their cars. We educate our teens about the importance of abstinence and safe sex to prevent STDs [sexually transmitted diseases]. And now we educate and warn them against smoking, even if we were smokers ourselves. With the evidence now available, simple prudence requires parents to prevent their children from using marijuana. Those parents who fail to do so are uninformed or irresponsible, or both.

We as parents need to face the facts about marijuana use, recognize that there is now compelling scientific evidence that was not available years ago and that the marijuana available to our children and teens is more dangerous as well. Parents are the most powerful prevention resource we have. But we need to take other action as well. Doctors, teachers, school officials, clergy and others who work with children and teens need to be alert to signs of marijuana use, intervene early and get help fast and to educate the country about the dangers of teen marijuana use, we need a national public education campaign.

We can use our law enforcement system too. I am not suggesting that we put kids in jail the first time they get caught smoking marijuana. But why not treat a teen arrested for marijuana use much the same way we treat someone arrested for drunk driving when no injury occurs and require them to attend sessions to learn about the dangers of marijuana use and how to decline the next time they are offered a joint? Why not use the arrest as an opportunity and require kids cited for marijuana possession or other offenses where marijuana is involved to be screened for substance use and other psychological problems and referred for help if appropriate?

We owe it to our children to use all the powers we have to keep them safe.

10

The Harmfulness of Marijuana Use Is Exaggerated

Maia Szalavitz

Maia Szalavitz is a senior fellow at STATS, a media watchdog organization affiliated with George Mason University that investigates coverage of science and statistics. She is also a journalist who covers health, science, and public-policy issues.

Scare tactics have long been used in the war on drugs, despite research suggesting such tactics are ineffective and may even increase experimentation. Exaggerated claims about marijuana's dangers might also cause teens to disregard warnings about other, more dangerous drugs. In some misleading ad campaigns, correlations, *that is, statistical relationships, between marijuana use and mental illness (for example, schizophrenia and depression) are used to imply that marijuana* causes *mental illness—a highly controversial and disputed claim. Rates of schizophrenia have remained fairly constant throughout the world over long periods of time, despite vast differences in the rate of marijuana use. While marijuana could be very dangerous for those already predisposed to schizophrenia, this would not apply to the vast majority of marijuana users. Evidence that marijuana causes depression is even more ambiguous, with some studies even showing that marijuana seemed to be associated with* lower *levels of depression. Recent research has even cast doubt on the claim that marijuana causes lung cancer, further undermining the credibility of such negative ad campaigns. These misleading*

Maia Szalavitz, "The Return of Reefer Madness," salon.com, November 20, 2008. This article first appeared in Salon.com, at http://www.salon.com. An online version remains in the Salon archives. Reprinted with permission.

strategies are used because marijuana is by far the most commonly used illegal drug, and any reduction in its use creates the appearance that the war on drugs is succeeding.

Parents who read the *New York Times* or *Newsweek* this past summer could be forgiven for freaking out when they came across a full-page ad warning them about the effects of marijuana on their teenagers. If the kids were off somewhere sparking up a joint, the federally funded message seemed to say, they were at risk for severe mental illness. Were those parents hallucinating, or was Reefer Madness, long since debunked, suddenly a real problem to be reckoned with?

The latest salvo in the never-ending war on drugs, the ads, which also ran in magazines like the *Nation* and the *National Review*, bore a stark warning. Under the headline "Marijuana and Your Teen's Mental Health," the bold-faced subhead announced: "Depression. Suicidal Thoughts. Schizophrenia."

"If you have outdated perceptions about marijuana, you might be putting your teen at risk," the text went on. It warned that "young people who use marijuana weekly have double the risk of depression later in life" and that "marijuana use in some teens has been linked to increased risk for schizophrenia." It followed with the sneering question, "Still think marijuana's no big deal?"

The rhetoric is alarming. But the research data used to support the ad campaign is hazy at best. Though carefully worded, the campaign blurs the key scientific distinction between *correlation* and *causation*. The ad uses some correlations between marijuana use and mental illness to imply that the drug can cause madness and depression. Yet these conclusions are unproven by current research. And several leading researchers are highly skeptical of them.

Scare tactics in the war on drugs have been around at least as long as Harry J. Anslinger, the federal drug warrior of the 1930s famed for his ludicrous pronouncements about the dangers of marijuana. But they're widely regarded as ineffective in deterring teen drug use. In fact, some research suggests they may actually increase experimentation. If anything, experts say, the latest ad campaign's overblown claims could damage credibility with teens, undermining warnings about other, more dangerous illicit substances. With medical marijuana a matter of renewed national debate, and with evidence emerging that there may be no connection between marijuana and lung cancer—a key strike against the drug's use in the past—the government's new campaign smacks more of desperation than science.

Spearheaded by the Office of National Drug Control Policy, better known as the "drug czar's" office, the ad campaign ran in print during May and June, it continues today on the federal government's Web site, Parents: The Anti-drug. There are plans to roll out more print, television and radio ads, according to an ONDCP spokesperson, if Congress approves the agency's current $150 million appropriations request this month.

The rhetoric [in antidrug ads] is alarming. But the research data used . . . is hazy at best.

At the press conference launching the mental illness campaign in May, the Bush administration's drug czar, John Walters, emphasized, "New research being conducted here and abroad illustrates that marijuana use, particularly during the teen years, can lead to depression, thoughts of suicide, and schizophrenia."

While the launch was attended by a former director of the National Institute on Drug Abuse, the current occupant of the office, Dr. Nora Volkow, did not attend or speak, nor did her deputies. This is unusual: The National Institute on Drug Abuse is the federal agency responsible for scientific research on the medical effects of drugs, so a campaign about marijuana's health effects would ordinarily feature at least one top representative discussing the science. The agency's name does not appear on the list of organizations endorsing the ad.

David Murray, special assistant in the drug czar's office, says that the National Institute on Drug Abuse was "involved in every aspect" of the planning of the campaign and "cleared and vetted" the statements in the ad and on the Web site. He says the drug czar's office didn't want to include more than one federal agency in the endorsements, adding that Volkow was out of the country at the time of the launch.

"Our research provides most of the evidence undergirding the campaign and we certainly support its goals," says Dr. Wilson Compton, director of the Division of Epidemiology, Services and Prevention Research at the National Institute on Drug Abuse. But Compton concedes that the findings cited in the ad are "not completely established" and that experts consider them "controversial" and worth further investigation.

According to Murray, the latest available data shows that the consumption of cannabis is a key risk factor for the development of serious mental illness. With regard to schizophrenia, the campaign cites one study of nearly 50,000 Swedish soldiers between the ages of 18 and 20, published in the *British Medical Journal* in 2002, which found that those who had smoked pot more than 50 times had a rate of schizophrenia nearly seven times as high as those who did not use marijuana at all.

The American Psychiatric Association is one of the major groups backing the campaign; a spokesperson referred to part of the group's policy statement as the reason for its endorsement: "The American Psychiatric Association is concerned and opposed to the use of drugs and alcohol in children."

Yet leading experts in psychiatric epidemiology (whom the APA recommended contacting, but who do not officially speak for the organization) are far from convinced about causal connections between marijuana and serious mental illness.

One key problem, they say, is that it's very difficult to determine whether pot smoking predisposes people to schizophrenia or whether early symptoms of schizophrenia predispose people to smoking pot—or whether some third factor causes some people to be more vulnerable to both.

In the Swedish study, for example, when factors already known to increase risk for schizophrenia were removed, such as a childhood history of disturbed behavior, the connection between marijuana use and risk for the disease was substantially reduced. Just one or two additional unknown influences could potentially wipe out the apparent marijuana-schizophrenia link, according to Dr. William Carpenter, a professor of psychiatry and pharmacology at the University of Maryland. Carpenter noted in a letter published in the *British Journal of Psychiatry* in October 2004 that the same genes that predispose someone to schizophrenia might also predispose them to substance abuse, but that drug use might start earlier simply because many people start using drugs in their teen years, while schizophrenia most commonly begins in the early 20s.

Perhaps the strongest piece of evidence to cast doubt on a causal connection between marijuana and schizophrenia is a long flat-line trend in the disease. While marijuana use rose from virtually nil in the 1940s and '50s to a peak period of use in 1979—when some 60 percent of high school seniors had tried it—schizophrenia rates remained virtually constant over those decades. The same remains true today: One percent or fewer people have schizophrenia, a rate consistent among populations around the world. This is in stark contrast to studies linking tobacco smoking with lung cancer, where rises in tobacco use were accompanied by rising rates of lung cancer.

"If anything, the studies seem to show a possible decline in schizophrenia from the '40s and the '50s," says Dr. Alan Brown, a professor of psychiatry and epidemiology at Columbia University. "If marijuana does have a causal role in schizophrenia, and that's still questionable, it may only play a role in a small percent of cases."

Even if today's kids are smoking more potent stuff, they don't get higher than their folks did.

For the tiny proportion of people who are at high risk for schizophrenia (those with a family history of the illness, for example), experts are united in thinking that marijuana could pose serious danger. For those susceptible, smoking marijuana could determine when their first psychotic episode occurs, and how bad it gets. A study published in 2004 in the *American Journal of Psychiatry* of 122 patients admitted to a Dutch hospital for schizophrenia for the first time found that, at least in men, marijuana users had their first psychotic episode nearly seven years earlier than those who did not use the drug. Because the neurotransmitters affected by marijuana are in brain regions known to be important to schizophrenia, there is a plausible biological mechanism by which marijuana could harm people prone to the disorder. Both Brown and Carpenter say that people with schizophrenia who smoke pot tend to have longer and more frequent psychotic episodes, and find it very difficult to quit using the drug.

Of course, the U.S. government's current ad campaign targets a much broader population than those highly vulnerable to schizophrenia, fanning fears based on a statistically rare scenario.

The campaign also declares that today's pot is more potent than the pot smoked by previous generations, implying heightened risk. Fine sinsemilla may seem more prevalent than ditchweed nowadays, but there is debate over whether today's average smoker is puffing on stronger stuff than the average stoner of the 1970s, as Daniel Forbes detailed in *Slate*. And, as Forbes showed, the drug czar's office has grossly exaggerated the numbers on this issue in the past.

Meanwhile, UCLA public policy expert Mark Kleiman has pointed out that federally funded research by the University of Michigan shows that since the 1970s the level of high reported by high school seniors who smoked marijuana has remained "flat as a pancake." In other words, even if today's kids are smoking more potent stuff, they don't get higher than their folks did—like drinking a few whiskey shots rather than multiple mugs of beer, they use less of the good stuff to achieve the same effect.

With regard to depression, evidence of a causal role for marijuana is even murkier. In general, depression rates in the population did rise sharply during the time period in which marijuana use also skyrocketed. But there were so many other relevant sociological factors that marked the last half of the 20th century—rising divorce rates, the changing roles of women, economic shifts, and better diagnoses of psychiatric conditions, to name a few—that scientists have rarely focused on marijuana as a potential cause for the increase in depression.

Murray maintains that scientists have simply overlooked marijuana in their search for explanations. One study published in the *Archives of General Psychiatry* in 2002, by New York University psychiatry professor Judith Brook and several colleagues, found that early marijuana use increased the risk of major depression by 19 percent. But that's not a substantial amount, according to Brook. And though the association remained after other factors were controlled for, such as living in poverty, it weakened further. "I wouldn't say that it's causal," Brook says. "It's an association. It appears to contribute."

The campaign selectively uses another piece of data, citing an Australian study published in the *British Medical Journal* in 2002 to assert that for teens, weekly marijuana use doubles the risk of depression. What that study found was that the risk doubled for teens who smoke marijuana weekly *or more frequently*. And it found that depression rates increased substantially in girls but not in boys. It also noted that "questions remain about the level of association between cannabis use and depression and anxiety and about the mechanism underpinning the link."

Moreover, a June 2005 study by researchers at University of Southern California, using the Center for Epidemiologic Studies' Depression Scale, found that marijuana use was in fact associated with *lower levels* of depression. Because the research was conducted using an Internet survey, it's possible that the most severely depressed people did not participate; nonetheless the study of more than 4,400 people found that both heavy pot smokers and moderate users reported less depression than did nonusers.

Dr. Myrna Weissman, a psychiatrist and leading epidemiologist of depression at Columbia University, sums up the current research and her view of marijuana's role in depression rates this way: "I can't imagine that it's a major factor."

The distortion of science under the Bush administration is, of course, nothing new.

"This is just more red-state culture-war politics," says UCLA's Kleiman, of the latest anti-marijuana campaign. He notes that since the government measures success in the war on drugs by a reduction in the number of drug users—rather than by declines in drug-related harm or addiction—marijuana is the obvious drug to go after. According to the most recent National Survey on Drug Use and Health from 2003, approximately 25 million Americans reported using marijuana over the previous year; compared with approximately 6 million users of cocaine and 1 million users of methamphetamine—both far more addictive substances—marijuana is a big, soft target.

Yet, for a public desensitized to fear-mongering antidrug messages, a campaign touting selected statistics from tenuous studies seems especially tone deaf, if not irresponsible.

The new study . . . found no connection between pot smoking—even by heavy users—and lung cancer.

"If I tell my 15-year-old that he's going to have a psychotic episode if he smokes pot, but he knows that his older brother already smokes pot and is fine, is he going to believe me when I tell him that methamphetamine damages the brain?" asks Mitch Earleywine, an associate professor of psychology at the State University of New York at Albany, who coauthored the USC study. Amphetamine psychosis is an established effect of taking large doses of that class of drugs; warnings about it appear on the labeling of prescription amphetamines. "What's going to happen," says Earleywine, "is we're going to lose all credibility with our teens."

The drug czar's office may soon face a full-blown credibility problem of its own regarding its fight against marijuana. Drug warriors have always had at least one powerful argument to fall back on when other attacks against marijuana seem to go up in smoke—but in the face of a new study, that may no longer be the case.

Previous research has pointed to the notion that smoking marijuana could cause cancer, the same way tobacco smoking has been incontrovertibly linked with cancer and death. The Institute of Medicine, charged by Congress with settling scientific debates, said in its last major report on the subject in 1999 that the fact that most users smoke marijuana is a primary reason to oppose its use as medicine.

But that reasoning was called into question in late June, when Dr. Donald Tashkin of the UCLA School of Medicine presented a large, case-control study—of the kind that have linked tobacco use with increases in lung cancer—at an annual scientific meeting of the International Cannabinoid Research Society in Clearwater, Fla. Tashkin is no hippie-dippy marijuana advocate: His earlier work has been cited by the drug czar's office itself, because his research showed that marijuana can cause lung damage. The new study, however, found no connection between pot smoking—even by heavy users— and lung cancer. In fact, among the more than 1,200 people studied, those who had smoked marijuana, but not cigarettes, appeared to have a lower risk for lung cancer than even those who had smoked neither.

The new research has not yet been peer reviewed, but it appears congruent with earlier studies that found no link between marijuana and increased cancer risk. If the data holds up to further scrutiny and testing, one can only speculate what new ad campaign the drug czar's office might cook up. Marijuana may not make most people crazy, but this latest discovery could really drive the old drug warriors bonkers.

11

Marijuana Prohibition Is Harmful

Gary Cartwright

Gary Cartwright is a newspaper reporter, a staff writer for Texas Monthly, *and the author of several books.*

Because politicians refuse to recognize that the war on drugs has been lost, they consistently block practical legislation that would reduce drug-related harm. Having decided years ago that marijuana is a menace, the government has been consistently misleading the public and the media by exaggerating claims of its harmfulness and denying its well-established reputation as a useful medicine. The war on drugs is being waged for political rather than scientific reasons, and some of the smartest people in America—including prominent conservatives—have called for an end to this enormous policy disaster. Legalizing marijuana and other drugs would drastically reduce the crime rate and make it much harder for children to obtain drugs.

What is it about marijuana that makes politicians halluci-nate? The faintest whiff of "the weed of madness" (as government propaganda used to call it) causes them to see distorted images of things that aren't there and never were: law and order, justice, reelection. But they don't see the obvi-ous. The war on drugs was lost years ago, and pretending oth-erwise only makes the problem worse. Consider the two marijuana-related bills that were introduced in the Texas Leg-islature during the 2005 session—each eminently practical,

Gary Cartwright, "Weed All About It," *Texas Monthly*, vol. 33, July 1, 2005, pp. 86, 88, 99. Copyright © 2005 Texas Monthly, Inc. Reproduced by permission.

neither with serious downsides, and both essentially dead on arrival. The first, written by Democratic state representative Harold Dutton, of Houston, would have reduced the penalty for possession of small amounts of marijuana. It was approved by the House Committee on Criminal Jurisprudence but never reached the floor for debate or a vote. In Texas, 97 percent of all marijuana arrests are for simple possession—an ounce or less—at a cost to taxpayers of $480 million a year. (Full disclosure: In 1968 I was arrested for possession of about two ounces of pot, which at the time could have meant life in prison; the charges were dropped after my lawyer got the search warrant thrown out.) In America, we spend nearly $8 billion trying to enforce the laws prohibiting the use and possession of marijuana. All we get for our money is a huge increase in organized crime, an endless string of drug-related murders, and the highest incarceration rate in the civilized world. The second bill, which was written by several House members, including Republican Terry Keel and Democrat Elliot Naishtat, both of Austin, would have facilitated the use of medical marijuana, or "medi-pot." It never got out of committee, even though there is ample evidence that smoking pot eases pain and reduces nausea associated with cancer, AIDS, multiple sclerosis, and other illnesses; it may also have a role in combating heart disease and strokes. The medi-pot bill was simple and straightforward—so elementary, in fact, that it was probably unworkable. It didn't legalize marijuana, but it did allow doctors to discuss it as an option with their patients and provided an affirmative defense for patients who are busted for following doctor's orders. But it didn't address, for example, how and where patients could obtain this still-illegal substance.

Increasing Public Acceptance of Medical Marijuana

A number of witnesses in wheelchairs appeared before the committee in April [2005], admitting that they regularly violated drug laws and explaining that marijuana in its natural form was the only drug that relieved their suffering. Chris Cain, a 36-year-old quadriplegic who has smoked pot for twelve years to control pain and spasms, described how his home near Beaumont was raided by a team of Hardin County sheriff's deputies with the assistance of two helicopters; they seized a small amount of marijuana and the computer equipment he uses to run his Internet business, then threw him in jail without regard to his need for medical attention. "I'm just asking for a fair trial," Cain told committee members. "I'm now a university graduate and a successful businessman. Marijuana has not damaged my brain, but it has made me a criminal."

Polls show that 75 percent of Texans support medical marijuana, and they're not the only ones. As of February [2005], ten states had adopted laws permitting the use of medi-pot (although in June, the U.S. Supreme Court ruled that medipot users can be federally prosecuted), and thirty had recognized its therapeutic potential. Still, the response to it here is mixed at best. One member of the committee, Democratic state representative Juan Escobar, of Kingsville, spent his career fighting drugs as a border patrolman and, later, as the head of an anti-drug task force. Nevertheless, Escobar is so convinced that medical marijuana makes sense that he supported it. Keel, a former county sheriff, told his fellow lawmakers: "We have, for some reason in our pharmacology, isolated that particular herb as not of medical value when, in fact, it is." Yet Democratic state representative Aaron Peña, of Edinburg, whose vote the bill's sponsors had counted on, couldn't bring himself to back it. He acknowledges that the drug war is lost. "All we're doing is loading up our prisons and burdening our taxpayers," he told me. "We need a paradigm shift toward treatment and education, and we need it fast." Ever since his sixteen-year-old son died four years ago of a drug overdose, however, he has dedicated himself to keeping kids off the stuff. "If I voted for it," he said, "how could I keep telling them that drugs are harmful?"

Marijuana has been used medically for hundreds of years and was prescribed by doctors in the U.S. until the thirties.

The Public Is Being Mislead

Though marijuana has been used medicinally for hundreds of years and was prescribed by doctors in the U.S. until the thirties, the government decided years ago that weed is a menace. In 1933 the feds launched their famous "reefer madness" campaign under Harry Anslinger, the zealous federal narcotics commissioner who supplied bogus information to the media that marijuana was responsible for insanity and violence. A federal law enacted in 1937 put marijuana in the same category as cocaine and opium. In 1970 Congress passed the Comprehensive Drug Abuse Prevention and Control Act, grouping marijuana with heroin as a narcotic with no medical use. In 1988 the Drug Enforcement Administration's chief law judge declared that "marijuana, in its natural form, is one of the safest therapeutically active substances known to man" and ruled that it be made available to doctors, but the agency ignored him.

Over time, law enforcement officials have repeatedly misled the public and the media about the so-called scourge of drugs. General Barry McCaffrey, Bill Clinton's drug czar, should have known better when he told the *Washington Post* in April 2000 that "illegal drugs will cost the United States 500,000 deaths . . . over the next decade." A twenty-year study by the Centers for Disease Control and Prevention shows that from 1979 through 1998, illegal drugs were the cause of just over 44,000 deaths, compared with the 380,000 poor souls whose deaths could be tied to alcohol. Meanwhile, George W.

Bush's drug czar, John Walters, has used his office to lobby against medical marijuana programs in various states. With increasing frequency, federal narcotics enforcers have conducted raids on growing operations. Even accepting the fact that the war on drugs has been waged for political rather than scientific ends, with arrest and imprisonment preferable to treatment and education, how could policy makers ignore something as benign as medi-pot? A cynic might suggest that their motive is to appease the far right, which has a pathological fear that some terminally ill wretch might smoke a little boo and break out in giggles.

Conservative Support for Legalization

Finding ourselves in such a monstrous hole, you'd hope someone would suggest we stop digging—and someone has. Several someones, in fact: a few of the smartest people in America, many of them conservative Republicans. Among those who have championed the legalization of marijuana are [prominent American author and conservative commentator] William F. Buckley. Nobel prize-winning economist Milton Friedman, former U.S. secretary of state George Shultz, and former New Mexico governor Gary Johnson. In his keynote address at the Fifth International Conference on Drug Policy Reform, in 1991, Friedman said that the country should admit that drug prohibition is a policy disaster, just as we once conceded as much for the prohibition of alcohol. The war on drugs and the harm it does, he has written, are "manifestations of a much broader problem: the substitution of political mechanisms for market mechanisms . . ." It has failed, he contends, because it's a "socialist enterprise" that is inefficient, expensive, and very advantageous to a small group of people—in this case, the drug enforcement agencies for whom the war is a raison d'être and the druglords whose cartels are a byproduct of U.S. policy.

Another conservative Republican who thinks prohibition is a dumb idea is the "right-wing-nutcase" I wrote about . . . [in March 2005] my pal Dr. Robert McFarlane. The Harvard-educated cardiologist has written dozens of letters and e-mails to politicians and friends arguing that drugs should be treated as a public health problem rather than a criminal matter. In an essay published in the *Palestine [Texas] Herald-Press* in March, Doc wrote: "By legalizing drugs, the profitability in their sale would evaporate, which would, in one stroke, eliminate everywhere the incentive to grow poppies and thus end the narco-wars in Afghanistan and Colombia . . . [and] would drastically lower the crime rate here and empty out our prisons." In recent months Doc has forwarded me news items about drug-related murders and reports of conversations with fellow wingnuts. After his piece ran in the *Herald-Press*, one conservative judge told him, "Heresy is just the truth spoken prematurely." A top Republican strategist confessed to Doc that his plan had merit but thought drug laws ought to stay on the books "because people are weak."

Making drugs illegal doesn't keep them out of the hands of kids.

Personal Responsibility

That nanny instinct, so at odds with traditional Republican dogma, is one of the arguments made by a conservative couple from Houston, Bob and Ann Lee, who for years have waged a campaign to legalize marijuana. "Current drug policies violate Republican philosophy of personal responsibility," the Lees wrote in a widely distributed pamphlet that rebuts many of the arguments advanced by drug warriors. They come to the subject with a heavy heart: Their son Richard is in a wheelchair, paralyzed from the waist down since a work accident damaged his spinal column in 1990. Legal drugs had serious side effects, so Richard turned to pot, at which point his parents discovered that most of what the government had told them about it wasn't true.

Exposing government lies is the easy part—and making drugs illegal doesn't keep them out of the hands of kids. Schoolchildren can't buy hard liquor, but hard drugs are as available as candy on the black market. Would legalization increase drug use? Maybe. But the use of tobacco, probably the most lethal drug today, has dramatically decreased because of intense anti-smoking campaigns. Some people will use drugs no matter what the consequences, but as Friedman and others point out, the user primarily harms himself. When he harms others, we do something about it, just as we arrest those who drink and drive. We arrest them not for the act of drinking but for the act of driving drunk.

Ending the war on drugs will take time, but politicians need to show some backbone. They should do what's best for America and ignore the fringe types who won't be happy until they're again allowed to burn witches. In the words of philosopher Robert Nozick, they should legalize "capitalist acts between consenting adults" and trust the free market they're always raving about.

12

Marijuana Users Need to Be Held Accountable for Their Actions

Ross Clark

Ross Clark is a journalist and columnist in the United Kingdom for The Spectator, The Times *and the* Sunday Telegraph.

Attitudes about marijuana have become increasingly liberal, and regardless of how it is legally classified, young people who are caught using the drug rarely face serious consequences, unlike the strict punishments of the past. Marijuana is a very harmful drug, and we should not be so tolerant of its use. People who become addicted to marijuana or other drugs have made a choice to use them, rather than being helpless victims as they are often portrayed. Liberal policies toward drug use have failed, and it is time to take sterner measures. Users must be held accountable for their actions and treated more harshly in order to discourage marijuana use.

After some consideration I am not sure that I can get excited about the debate as to whether cannabis should be classified as a Class B drug or whether, as the [British] Home Secretary Charles Clarke decided ... [in January 2006] it should remain Class C [In Britain, illegal drugs are classified as Class C, Class B, or Class A according to how dangerous they are considered to be, and therefore how harsh the punishment for misuse will be; Class A is considered most dangerous, Class C least dangerous. In May 2008, a decision was made to move marijuana from Class C to Class B.]. Rather, I am coming round to the conclusion that is should be declassified as a drug altogether—and reclassified as a banned foodstuff. Instead of being handled by a bunch of creepy do-gooders from the drugs' charities, the battle to keep it off the streets would then be run by the zealots of the Food Standards Agency [a British government department in charge of food safety]. You wouldn't get dopeheads and smalltime dealers being let off with a caution on the grounds that it isn't fair to burden young people with a criminal record: they would be heavily fined, branded a danger to the public and named and shamed in the local papers. Just ask any former sandwich bar-owner who was imprudent enough to serve an egg sandwich made with mayonnaise that was a few days out of date.

Increasing Tolerance Toward Marijuana

Whether cannabis is Class B or Class C is an irrelevance. Technically, the difference is whether users can be jailed for two or five years. But it hardly matters, given that few people are prosecuted for using drugs anyway. Do middle-class types passing round weed at south London parties really fear that a copper passing their window might sniff the evidence and get them banged up for a couple of years? I think not. When I was at school in the early 1980s the only boy ever caught with cannabis in school was summarily expelled: any state school head who applied the same punishment now would provoke horror among liberal-minded parents. With columnists openly boasting of their drug habits and attempting to make out that anyone like me who has never taken illegal drugs is an odd-ball, the laws against drug-taking have become reduced to the same status as the law against hanging your washing out on a Monday morning or failing to engage in two hours' archery practice: they are treated as some quaint hangover from an earlier age.

I wish I could share the libertarian view that cannabis is either a harmless bit of fun or, inasmuch as it does damage the health, it is the individual's right to choose whether to take the risk or not. But I'm sorry, I can't. I don't think it is a good idea that a drug which promotes mental illness, and the life-long misery which that entails, should be tolerated. And yes, the state does have a right to ban dangerous substances. After all, drug libertarians are rarely libertarian when it comes to dealing with the consequences of addiction. They don't tend to look at some junkie shrivelled up on the pavement, shrug their shoulders and say, 'Oh, well, it was the silly bugger's fault for getting himself into trouble; it is no business of the state to intervene.' Rather, they want all the drug rehabilitation centres which public money can provide. I am not against re-hab, but if the state is going to pick drug-addicts up and give them a second chance, surely it has every right to impose laws to prevent people falling into drug addiction in the first place?

The most comprehensive study . . . found that cannabis doubled the risk of developing schizophrenia.

Marijuana Is Harmful to Mental Health

As regards the issue of whether cannabis really does cause mental illness, I am not convinced by the statistic, produced . . .[in January 2006] by the Home Office's advisory council on misuse of drugs, that 'at worst, using cannabis increases the lifetime risk of developing schizophrenia by 1 per cent'. That is a very loaded way of presenting the evidence. The most comprehensive study on the subject, published by Professor Robin Murray in the *British Journal of Psychiatry*, found that cannabis doubled the risk of developing schizophrenia. Unlike, say, tobacco, where the risks of succumbing to illness increase progressively with age, the dope-smokers who develop schizophrenia are depressingly young. Moreover, the issue of schizophrenia and cannabis, which has dominated the debate over the past week, ignores the numerous depressives and non-schizophrenic paranoiacs who have been reduced to their condition by dope.

I wasn't party to the advisory council's discussions, but looking at the complexion of the committee I cannot say I am surprised at its decision to keep cannabis a Class C drug. Its scientists are outnumbered by social workers from rehab charities: advocates, in other words, of drug-users. It has a solitary policeman but no parent of a youth reduced to a gibbering wreck by cannabis nor a representative from a community which has to live with the results of a liberal drugs policy. The experts called to give evidence included only one foreign politician, who funnily enough came from Holland, which has practised a liberal approach to drugs for a generation. Of course he should be listened to, but why didn't the council want to hear about the experience of countries which have practised a tougher attitude to cannabis? The philosophy which emanates from the report is one which has ruled discussion of drugs for years: that drug-users are essentially victims who must under no circumstances be punished because that will only make their problems worse. Of course, these evil drugs traffickers from darkest South America must be tackled, runs this philosophy, but the users themselves must be treated with nothing but love and understanding. It is a view shared not just on the Left but increasingly, too, in Conservative circles. Indeed, it was typified by [British Conservative Party head] David Cameron's admission that a close relative of his 'has had a dreadful problem with drugs'. 'They have come through it,' he added, 'been through rehabilitation and I'm incredibly proud of them.'

Maybe I come from some cruel Protestant background and am entirely unsuited to life in touchy-feely New Britain, but I find it hard to sympathise with the view that junkies are poor innocents who are helplessly swept into their drug habit.

That is perhaps true of a council-block child brought up by a heroin-addict parent. But in the case of somebody from David Cameron's background, my first instinct is not pride that the addict has beaten the habit: it is shame that they ever developed it in the first place. Making 'victims' out of people who are authors of their own downfall seems to me merely to encourage young attention-seekers into taking drugs.

Harsher Punishments Needed for Marijuana Use

The decriminalisation lobby often argues that the 'war on drugs' has failed and therefore something else must be tried. But what war on drugs? There is little point hectoring the heads of South American nations to crack down on the suppliers when their British customers go unpunished. When faced with prostitution and child pornography, the government doesn't shrink from prosecuting the customers: they don't get treated as helpless victims of an evil trade. On the contrary, they are held to be every bit as guilty as the suppliers.

Making 'victims' out of people who are authors of their own downfall seems to me merely to encourage young attention-seekers into taking drugs.

I am not advocating that drug-users be sent to jail, as the law still technically allows. Clearly, it would be bone-headed to send a young dope-smoker into an environment where he will merely gain an introduction to the harder stuff. But I never really understood what was wrong with [British Conservative Party politician] Ann Widdecombe's suggestion, at a Conservative Party conference a few years ago, that anyone caught with cannabis be subjected to an instant fine. I have no particular liking for the former shadow home secretary, but I found the contempt heaped upon her by libertarian members of her own party disgusting. You break the law, you get punished in a proportionate way; since when did that cease to be a principle of Conservative thought? So far, the government's main contribution to the 'war' against cannabis has been a large tax concession to the makers of a 'feel-good' movie called *Saving Grace*, which makes a heroine out of a cannabis-grower. It isn't a 'war' against drugs which has failed, but a liberal approach. Unless we want our psychiatric hospitals overflowing, perhaps it is time potential drug-users were dissuaded from the habit under threat of being fined, expelled from schools and jobs, forced into rehab, regarded with moderate shame and generally treated as the criminals they still, technically, would be.

13

Common Sense Is Needed in Marijuana Policy

Cathy Young

Cathy Young is a contributing editor at Reason *magazine, and her column appears regularly in the* Boston Globe.

The demonization of drugs has created a situation that is just as dangerous as drug abuse itself, leading to the persecution of medical marijuana users and highly oppressive laws similar to those in the old Soviet Union. Both the Republican and the Democratic parties have betrayed their own principles in pursuing the drug war. Decriminalization of drug use by adults would respect the right of people to make their own decisions and would reduce many of the drug-associated problems faced by society. Legalization may be going too far, but it is time to reduce the hysteria around drug use and look for practical solutions to this problem.

With everything else going on in the world, it's good to know that the federal government is being vigilant when it comes to the *really* dangerous people: those unrepentant chronic-pain patients who viciously insist on using marijuana to relieve their suffering. Last week [June 2005] in *Gonzales v. Raich*, the Supreme Court ruled that federal drug laws supersede the laws several states have passed in recent years legalizing the production and use of marijuana for medicinal purposes. Apparently, the actions of a sick woman in California growing pot in her basement for her medical needs affect "in-

Cathy Young, "The Medical Pot Hysteria," boston.com, June 13, 2005. Reproduced by permission of the author.

terstate commerce," which means that the Constitution says it's all right to bring in the feds.

The ruling is bad legal reasoning; commentators such as Boston University law professor Randy Barnett, who argued the case before the Supreme Court . . . [in November 2004] point out that it directly contradicts several of the court's decisions in recent years narrowing the scope of federal powers. It is also bad moral reasoning. Whether you use personal autonomy or compassion as your standard, denying seriously ill men and women access to a drug that could help them is repugnant.

Moreover, as Dr. Sally Satel, a psychiatrist and resident scholar at the American Enterprise Institute, writes in the *New York Times*, research on therapeutic uses of marijuana has been held back by ideologically motivated restrictions.

Decriminalization would take drug profits for organized crime and even terrorism out of the equation.

Dangerous Demonization of Drugs

All this is the latest example of how the war on drugs has addled our brains. Yes, drug abuse is a serious problem. But the demonization of illegal drugs—even mild ones such as marijuana, which tens of millions of Americans have indulged in with consequences no worse than for legal intoxicants—has created a climate that is just as dangerous.

The persecution of medical marijuana users is one example. Here's another: Under a congressional bill proposed by Republican Representative James Sensenbrenner of Wisconsin, if you are aware of any drug use or sale on a college campus or in a home with children and fail to report it within 24 hours, you will face a minimum two-year prison sentence. Maybe we could call it Uncle Joe's Law, since it has a distinct flavor of the [Joseph] Stalin-era Soviet Union where people could be imprisoned for failing to report political crimes. I'm not fond of Soviet parallels for the actions of democratic government, but this parallel does suggest itself. It's all the more galling since this proposed Draconian measure is not directed at terrorists who want to kill us, but at college kids who want a few hits of pot.

This isn't a conservative-versus-liberal, Republican-versus-Democrat issue: Both parties are drug war parties. (It was the Clinton administration in the 1990s that decided to use federal authority to thwart new state laws legalizing medical marijuana: In 1996, Clinton approved a plan to subject doctors who prescribe the drug to federal prosecution.) It's hard to tell which side is more guilty of hypocrisy. What happened to the conservatives' commitment to the principles of states' rights and limited government? What happened to liberals' concern for the rights of defendants and to the right to privacy?

Pragmatic Reasons for Legalization

The libertarian solution to this problem is to legalize or at least decriminalize drug use, at least for adults. There are solid arguments for this: In a free society, people should generally be able to decide what substances they put in their bodies. On a pragmatic level, decriminalization would take drug profits for organized crime and even terrorism out of the equation. The obvious counterargument is that it will lead to more drug abuse, since obtaining drugs will be far easier. But the most likely result would be a small increase in casual use: when drugs are illegal, it stands to reason that the kind of people who obtain them are also more prone to addiction. Drug prohibition is based on the idea that the diabolical power of drugs robs people of the ability to make choices. Yet, as Satel persuasively argued earlier this month at an American Enterprise Institute conference on neuroscience and morality, this isn't true: addicts can and do choose to quit.

Satel believes that marijuana should be treated no differently from alcohol, with generally tougher drunk driving penalties. However, she does not support drug legalization; for one, she told me, it is a political nonstarter that diverts attention from practical solutions (such as more emphasis on treatment rather than prosecution). That's almost certainly true. But maybe we should start by just saying no to drug hysteria. Then, in a saner climate, we can start thinking about solutions.

Organizations to Contact

The editors have compiled the following list of organizations concerned with the issues debated in this book. The descriptions are derived from materials provided by the organizations. All have publications or information available for interested readers. The list was compiled on the date of publication of the present volume; the information provided here may change. Be aware that many organizations take several weeks or longer to respond to inquiries, so allow as much time as possible.

Americans for Safe Access (ASA)
1322 Webster Street, Suite 402, Oakland, CA   94612
(888) 929-4367
e-mail: info@safeaccessnow.org
Web site: www.safeaccessnow.org

Americans for Safe Access (ASA) works to protect the rights of patients and doctors to use marijuana for medical purposes. ASA's mission is to ensure safe, legal access to marijuana for all who are helped by it. The organization provides legal training for lawyers and patients, medical information for doctors and patients, media support for court cases, and activist training to organizers.

Common Sense for Drug Policy (CSDP)
1377-C Spencer Avenue, Lancaster, PA   17603
(717) 299-0600 • fax: (717) 393-4953
e-mail: info@csdp.org
Web site: www.csdp.org

Common Sense for Drug Policy (CSDP) is a nonprofit organization dedicated to reforming drug policy. The organization disseminates factual information and comments on existing laws, policies, and practices. CSDP advocates the regulation and control of marijuana in a manner similar to alcohol and subject to local, rather than federal, decisions.

Drug Enforcement Administration (DEA)

Mailstop: AES, 8701 Morrissette Drive
Springfield, VA   22152
(202) 307-1000
Web site: www.dea.gov

The mission of the Drug Enforcement Administration is to enforce the controlled substances laws and regulations of the United States. It coordinates the activities of federal, state, and local agencies, and works with foreign governments to reduce the availability of illicit drugs in the United States.

Drug Free America Foundation

2600 9th Street, N, Suite 200, St. Petersburg, FL   33704-2744
(727) 828-0211 • fax: (727) 828-0212
Web site: www.dfaf.org

Drug Free America Foundation is a drug prevention and policy organization committed to developing, promoting, and sustaining global strategies, policies, and laws that will reduce illegal drug use, drug addiction, and drug-related injury and death. The organization believes that the legalization of marijuana would be harmful to society.

Drug Policy Alliance Network

925 15th Street, NW, 2nd Floor, Washington, DC   20005
(202) 216-0035 • fax: (202) 216-0803
e-mail: dc@drugpolicy.org
Web site: www.drugpolicy.org

The Drug Policy Alliance Network believes in the sovereignty of individuals over their minds and bodies. Its position is that people should be punished for crimes committed against others, but not for using marijuana or other drugs as a personal choice. It promotes alternatives to the war on drugs in the United States and works to reduce the harms of drug misuse.

Drug Reform Coordination Network

1623 Connecticut Avenue, NW, 3rd Floor
Washington, DC   20009
(202) 293-8340 • fax: (202) 293-8344
e-mail: drcnet@drcnet.org
Web site: stopthedrugwar.org

The Drug Reform Coordination Network is an organization of educators, students, lawyers, health care professionals, academics, and others working to reform current drug policies. The organization believes that the federal government should reschedule marijuana to permit medical use.

Erowid

P.O. Box 1116, Grass Valley, CA   95945
e-mail: sage@erowid.org
Web site: www.erowid.org

Erowid is a member-supported organization providing access to reliable, nonjudgmental information about psychoactive plants and chemicals and related issues. It posits that truth, accuracy, and integrity in publishing information about psychoactives will lead to healthier and more balanced choices, behaviors, and policies around all psychoactive medications, entheogens, herbs, and recreational drugs.

Marijuana Policy Project (MPP)

P.O. Box 77492, Capitol Hill, Washington, DC   20013
(202) 462-5747
e-mail: info@mpp.org
Web site: www.mpp.org

The Marijuana Policy Project (MPP) is the largest marijuana policy reform organization in the United States. MPP works to minimize the harm associated with marijuana—both the consumption of marijuana and the laws that are intended to prohibit such use. The organization believes that the greatest harm associated with marijuana is prison and focuses on removing criminal penalties for marijuana use. It also works to make marijuana medically available to seriously ill people who have the approval of their doctors.

Multidisciplinary Association for
Psychedelic Studies (MAPS)
10424 Love Creek Road, Ben Lomond, CA   95005
(831) 336-4325 • fax: (831) 336-3665
e-mail: askmaps@maps.org
Web site: maps.org

MAPS is a membership-based, nonprofit research and educational organization. It assists scientists to design, obtain approval for, fund, conduct, and report on research into the healing and spiritual potentials of psychedelics and marijuana. One of its priorities is to research the potential for marijuana to become an FDA-approved prescription medicine.

The National Center on Addiction and
Substance Abuse (CASA)
633 Third Avenue, 19th Floor, New York, NY   10017-6706
(212) 841-5200
Web site: www.casacolumbia.org

The National Center on Addiction and Substance Abuse (CASA) at Columbia University is the only national organization that brings together under one roof all the professional disciplines needed to study and combat abuse of all substances—alcohol, nicotine, illegal drugs, prescription drugs, performance-enhancing drugs—in all sectors of society.

National Institute on Drug Abuse (NIDA)
6001 Executive Boulevard, Room 5213
Bethesda, MD   20892-9561
(301) 443-1124
e-mail: information@nida.nih.gov
Web site: www.nida.nih.gov

The National Institute on Drug Abuse is one of the National Institutes of Health, a component of the U.S. Department of Health and Human Services. It supports scientific research on drug abuse and addiction. NIDA also works to disseminate the results of this research to policy makers, drug abuse practitioners, other health care practitioners, and the general public.

National Organization for the Reform of Marijuana Laws (NORML)

1600 K Street, NW, Suite 501, Washington, DC   20006-2832
(888) 676-6765 • fax: (202) 483-0057
e-mail: norml@norml.org
Web site: www.norml.org

NORML is a public-interest advocacy group that opposes marijuana prohibition. The organization supports the right of adults to use marijuana responsibly for both personal and medical purposes. It believes that all penalties should be eliminated for responsible use. Further, NORML believes that a legally regulated market should be established where consumers can buy marijuana in a safe and secure environment.

Office of National Drug Control Policy (ONDCP)

P.O. Box 6000, Rockville, MD   20849-6000
(800) 666-3332 • fax: (301) 519-5212
Web site: www.whitehousedrugpolicy.gov

The White House Office of National Drug Control Policy was established by the Anti-Drug Abuse Act of 1988. Its purpose is to establish policies, priorities, and objectives for the nation's drug control program. The goals of the program are to reduce illicit drug use, manufacturing, and trafficking; drug-related crime and violence; and drug-related health consequences.

RAND Drug Policy Research Center

1776 Main Street, Santa Monica, CA   90407-2138
(310) 393-0411 • fax: (310) 393-4818
e-mail: dprc@rand.org
Web site: www.rand.org

The RAND Corporation is a research institution that seeks to improve public policy through research and analysis. RAND's

Drug Policy Research Center disseminates information on the costs, prevention, and treatment of alcohol and drug abuse as well as on trends in drug-law enforcement.

**Substance Abuse and Mental Health
Services Administration (SAMHSA)**
1 Chock Cherry Road, Rockville, MD   20857
(240) 276-2000 • fax: (240) 276-2010
Web site: www.samhsa.gov

The Substance Abuse and Mental Health Services Administration (SAMHSA) has established a clear vision for its work—a life in the community for everyone. To realize this vision, the agency has sharply focused its mission on building resilience and facilitating recovery for people with or at risk for mental or substance-use disorders.

Bibliography

Books

Joan Bello and
Steve Willis

The Benefits of Marijuana: Physical, Psychological, and Spiritual, 3rd rev. ed. Boca Raton, FL: Lifeservices Press, 2007.

Martin Booth

Cannabis: A History. New York: Picador, 2005.

Jay Carter Brown

Smuggler's Blues: The Saga of a Marijuana Importer. Toronto: ECW Press, 2007.

Nick Brownlee

This Is Cannabis. London: Sanctuary, 2004.

Timmen L.
Cermak

Marijuana: What's a Parent to Believe? Center City, MN: Hazelden, 2003.

Mitch Earleywine

Understanding Marijuana: A New Look at the Scientific Evidence. New York: Oxford University Press, 2005.

David Emmett
and Graeme Nice

What You Need to Know About Cannabis: Understanding the Facts. London: Jessica Kingsley, 2009.

Hendrik Geels

The Blessed Herb: Medicinal Cannabis Users in Their Own Words. Charleston, SC: BookSurge, 2004.

Rudolph J. Gerber *Legalizing Marijuana: Drug Policy Reform and Prohibition Politics.* Westport, CT: Praeger, 2004.

Ted Gottfried *The Facts About Marijuana.* Tarrytown, NY: Benchmark Books, 2005.

Leslie L. Iversen *The Science of Marijuana.* New York: Oxford University Press, 2007.

James Langton *No Need for Weed: Understanding and Breaking Cannabis Dependency.* Hindsight, 2008.

Patrick Matthews *Cannabis Culture.* London: Bloomsbury UK, 2003.

Michael Poole *Romancing Mary Jane: A Year in the Life of a Failed Marijuana Grower.* Vancouver, British Columbia: Greystone Books, 2003.

Ed Rosenthal and Steve Kubby with S. Newhart *Why Marijuana Should Be Legal.* New York: Thunder's Mouth Press, 2003.

E.J. Sanna *Marijuana: Mind-Altering Weed.* Broomall, PA: Mason Crest, 2008.

Eric Schlosser *Reefer Madness: Sex, Drugs, and Cheap Labor in the American Black Market.* New York: Mariner Books, 2004.

Periodicals

Joseph V. Amodio "Why Pot's Not Cool: How Marijuana Messes with Your Brain and Body," *Current Health*, vol. 2, March 2005.

Sarah Baldauf "What Parents Need to Know About Pot," *U.S. News and World Report*, May 23, 2008.

Eve Bender "Twin Study Adds Fuel to Marijuana Debate," *Psychiatric News*, March 21, 2003.

Mark Borden "High Times," *Los Angeles Magazine*, April 2007.

Bill Breen "The Cannabis Conundrum: Medical Marijuana Could Be the Next Big Thing in Biotech, But Not in the United States," *Fast Company*, February 2004.

Elaine Briere "Da's Toch Dope, Man! The Dutch Decriminalization Debate Moves to the 'Back Door,'" *Briarpatch*, February 2008.

Monte Burke "Inside Dope," *Forbes*, March 26, 2007.

Deborah Crowe "Buzz Killed: L.A. Pot Shops See Budding Success Go Up in Smoke," *Los Angeles Business Journal*, February 11, 2008.

Daily Record (St. Louis, Mo.) "Family Marijuana Cases Stir Legalization Debate," June 17, 2006.

Denver Post	"It's Time to Rethink and Reform Drug Laws," September 5, 2004.
Charlie Gillis	"Thank You for Not Smoking Up: Canada's Drift Toward Legalizing Pot May Be Coming to a Halt," *Maclean's*, August 25, 2008.
Gary Greenberg	"Respectable Reefer: How a Pulverized, Liquefied, and Doctor-Prescribed Form of Marijuana Could Transform the Drug-War Landscape," *Mother Jones*, November 2005.
Quentin Hardy	"Inside Dope" [Canada's Marijuana Industry], *Forbes*, November 10, 2003.
Harvard Health Letter	"Reefer Rx: Marijuana as Medicine," September 2004.
Dan Hurley	"Medical Marijuana on Trial," *New York Times*, March 29, 2005.
Troy Johnson	"7 Reasons to Lay off the Weed (And Being a Dumbass Isn't One of Them)," *Surfer*, June 2006.
Scott Kirkwood	"A Growing Problem: Criminals Are Growing Marijuana in Sequoia and Yosemite National Parks, and the Impact Is Spreading Like Weeds," *National Parks*, Summer 2005.
Johnathan V. Last	"The Bitterest Pill; Europe Becomes Less Drug-Friendly," *Weekly Standard*, October 22, 2007.

Ethan A. Nadelmann	"An End to Marijuana Prohibition: The Drive to Legalize Picks Up," *National Review*, July 12, 2004.
Nina Riccio	"What You Should Know About Marijuana: Is It 'No Big Deal' or 'Big Trouble'?" *Current Health*, vol. 2, January 2003.
David Samuels	Dr. Kush: How Medical Marijuana Is Transforming the Pot Industry," *The New Yorker*, July 28, 2008.
Sally Satel	"A Whiff of 'Reefer Madness' in U.S. Drug Policy," *New York Times*, August 16, 2005.
U.S. News and World Report	"10 Questions Adolescents Have About Marijuana," April 25, 2008.
Marlize van Romburgh and Giana Magnoli	"Last Dance with Mary Jane, No More Time to Kill the Pain," *America's Intelligence Wire*, August 14, 2008.
John P. Walters	"No Surrender: The Drug War Saves Lives," *National Review*, September 27, 2004.

Index